THE W🌐RLD BANK and the ENVIRONMENT

Fiscal 1992

The World Bank
Washington, D.C.

This publication was prepared by World Bank staff, and the findings,
interpretations, and conclusions expressed in it do not necessarily represent the views of the Bank's Board of Executive Directors or the
countries they represent.

The text is printed on recycled paper that exceeds the requirements of
the 1988 guidelines of the U.S. Environmental Protection Agency, section
6002 of the Resource Conservation Recovery Act. The paper stock contains at least 50 percent recovered waste paper material as calculated by
fiber content, of which at least 10 percent of the total fiber is postconsu-
mer waste, and 20 to 50 percent of the fiber has been deinked.

ISBN 0-8213-2232-X
ISSN 1014-8132

Contents

Bibliography   144

Boxes

This report was prepared by by the Environment Department of the World
Bank in close collaboration with the regional Environment Divisions. Don
Hinrichsen, Marian Mabel, and Will Wade-Gery prepared the report under
the supervision of Mohamed T. El-Ashry and Andrew Steer.

Preface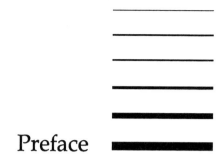

In 1987 the World Bank embarked on a major effort to incorporate environmental concerns into all aspects of its work. Progress reports were prepared for the Development Committee in 1987, 1988, and 1989. In 1990 it was decided to initiate a series of annual reports with the purpose of documenting progress and ensuring that the lessons of success and failure are put to good use.

This is the third annual report in the series. It sets out the Bank's principal environmental activities during fiscal 1992 (the period from July 1, 1991, to June 30, 1992) and its future initiatives, in the context of the findings and recommendations of *World Development Report 1992* and the agreements reached at the United Nations Conference on Environment and Development (the "Earth Summit").

Abbreviations and Acronyms

AFTEN	Africa Region, Environment Division (of the World Bank)
CFC	Chlorofluorocarbon
CGIAR	Consultative Group on International Agricultural Research
EA	Environmental assessment
EAP	Environmental action plan
ECE	United Nations Economic Commission for Europe
EDI	Economic Development Institute (of the World Bank)
EIA	Environmental impact assessment
EIB	European Investment Bank
EIS	Environmental information system
ESMAP	Energy Sector Management Assistance Program
GDP	Gross domestic product
GEF	Global Environment Facility
GIS	Geographic Information System
GNP	Gross national product
IBRD	International Bank for Reconstruction and Development
IDA	International Development Association
IFC	International Finance Corporation
IPM	Integrated pest management
IPPS	Industrial Pollution Projection System
MARPOL	Protocol on Prevention of Pollution from Ships
MEIP	Metropolitan Environmental Improvement Program
METAP	Mediterranean Environmental Technical Assistance Program
NGO	Nongovernmental organization
OECD	Organization for Economic Cooperation and Development
OED	Operations Evaluations Department (of the World Bank)
UMP	Urban Management Program
UNCED	United Nations Conference on Environment and Development ("Earth Summit")
UNCHS	United Nations Center for Human Settlements
UNDP	United Nations Development Programme
UNEP	United Nations Environment Programme

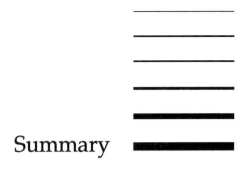

Summary

The past year has seen important progress in the World Bank's continuing efforts to incorporate environmental concerns into its work.[1] But the year was more than simply part of an ongoing process. The United Nations Conference on Environment and Development (UNCED) and the publication of *World Development Report 1992* hold important implications for the Bank's future work.

Bank activities during fiscal 1992 drew heavily on the accumulated experience and research of the past several years. During this period a set of principles and policies evolved that will guide future actions. The important events of 1992 can be thought of as marking the transition from the first phase, one of efforts to integrate the goals of environment and development, to a new phase in which particular attention will be given to the implementation of these policies, so that actions will more consistently correspond to agreed principles.

The World Bank's environmental activities, which involve policy dialogue, lending, technical assistance, research, and aid coordination, have four objectives:

- To assist member countries in setting priorities, building institutions, and implementing programs for sound environmental stewardship
- To ensure that potential adverse environmental impacts from Bank-financed projects are addressed
- To assist member countries in building on the complementarities between poverty reduction and environmental protection
- To address global environmental challenges through participation in the Global Environment Facility (GEF).

Assisting Countries with Environmental Management

Assisting member countries in their efforts to improve environmental management while accelerating development is the principal objective

1

of the Bank's environmental work. Governments seek the Bank's technical and financial support in developing national and sectoral strategies, in strengthening institutions, policy analysis and research, and in designing and implementing investment projects.

Environmental action plans (EAPs) are emerging as important vehicles for assisting borrowers to set environmental priorities and to map out ways of achieving them. They also facilitate better project selection and design, since they allow the Bank and other lending institutions and donors to focus support for investments in agreed-on priority areas.

To date, seven International Development Association (IDA) borrowers—Burkina Faso, the Arab Republic of Egypt, Ghana, Lesotho, Madagascar, Rwanda, and Sri Lanka—have completed EAPs. The Bank's role in the preparation and implementation of an EAP is primarily to provide advice and help arrange technical assistance, at the request of the government. Each action plan is unique, but common goals include: (a) furthering environmental policy and legislation; (b) strengthening the institutional framework for dealing with environmental issues; (c) building national capacity and developing human resources for carrying out environmental management; (d) establishing environmental monitoring and information systems; and (e) addressing the management of key natural resources such as soils, water, forests, fisheries, and energy.

The number of World Bank loans for environmental management, in direct support of country environmental priorities, continues to rise. Fiscal 1992 saw the approval of nineteen projects that were primarily environmental, with Bank financing of $1.2 billion.[2] Another forty-three projects contained significant environmental components. The Bank's Africa region had six major environmental projects, amounting to about $184 million, and eleven projects with significant components addressing environmental issues. The Asia and Pacific region had eight environmental projects, totaling $495 million, and sixteen projects with environmental components. The Europe and Central Asia region and the Middle East and North Africa region together had six projects with environmental components, and the Latin America and Caribbean region had five major environmental projects, amounting to almost $500 million, and ten projects with significant environmental components.

Lending increased notably for country-level institution building and for management of critical natural resources such as forests, watersheds, fresh water, wildlife, and soils. Of the major environmental projects approved in 1992, ten were primarily concerned with better management of natural resources and six with building institutional capacity to plan and implement environmental strategies and action plans. A number of projects focused on both priorities. For example,

- In Africa the $20 million Mali Natural Resource Management Project is designed to improve management of natural resources by strengthening the capacity of local communities to manage their own resources, improving the management capacity of the Ministry for Agriculture, Livestock, and the Environment, and supporting the development of a national environmental information system.
- In Asia the $124 million Maharashtra (India) Forestry Project supports integrated investments in the entire forestry sector, including soil and water conservation activities, wildlife preservation, agroforestry, and institution strengthening.
- In Latin America the Mato Grosso (Brazil) Natural Resources Management Project allocates $205 million for sustainable management of key resources such as watersheds, forests, fresh water, and minerals.

Environmental Assessment of Projects Supported by World Bank Loans

The Bank continues to strengthen its capacity to assess potential environmental impacts from projects it supports. Environmental assessment identifies ways of making projects more environmentally sustainable by preventing, minimizing, mitigating, or compensating for adverse impacts.

A new Operational Directive on Environmental Assessment, issued this fiscal year, requires Bank staff to classify investment projects into three broad environmental assessment categories on the basis of the potential environmental impact, which in turn determines the nature and extent of environmental analysis needed. For projects assigned to category A, a full environmental assessment is required. Examples include dams and reservoirs, industrial estates, large-scale irrigation and flood control, and land clearance. Projects placed in category B undergo environmental analysis but do not require a full environmental assessment. The impacts of category B projects are not likely to be as sensitive, numerous, or diverse as those of category A projects. Examples include small-scale agroindustry, aquaculture, rural electrification, watershed management, and rural water supply and sanitation. No environmental assessment or analysis is required for category C projects—family planning, education, health and nutrition, and the like—since they are unlikely to have adverse environmental effects.

After two years of experience with environmental assessments, the Bank has completed its first review of the environmental assessment process. As of the end of fiscal 1992, about thirty environmental assessment summaries had been presented to the Bank's Board of Executive Directors; of these, twenty summaries and eight full environmental assessments had been reviewed and evaluated by Bank staff. Although the Bank's environmental assessment procedures were found to be realistic, workable, and instrumental in improving development planning and environmental management, more effort is needed to strengthen borrowers' capacities to conduct effective environmental assessment. The report recommends that key borrowing countries be given high priority for EA training and that Bank resources devoted to environmental assessment be bolstered until borrowers' capacities have improved.

A notable event of fiscal 1992 was the report of the Independent Review for the Sardar Sarovar (Narmada) projects in India, commissioned in fiscal 1991 by Barber B. Conable, then president of the World Bank. The report reviewed the resettlement and environmental impacts of the projects and identified weaknesses in planning and implementation, including the lack of a resettlement strategy and the absence of a coordinated assessment of environmental impacts. It underscores the importance of good baseline data and of effective consultation of and participation by local people and the need for comprehensive environmental impact assessments and effective national and local environmental institutions.

Poverty Reduction and the Environment

Integral to sustainable development and the reduction of poverty is protection of the natural resource base on which development depends. The World Bank recognizes that promoting development and protecting the environment are complementary aspects of the same agenda. The Bank's effectiveness in combating poverty, while protecting the environment, is the benchmark by which its performance as a development institution should be judged.

The recently issued Operational Directive on Poverty Reduction and the "Poverty Reduction Handbook" are intended to guide staff in this task. They contain guidelines for and examples of best practice for implementing the Bank's poverty reduction strategy. The country poverty assessments required by the new operational directive provide the basis for a collaborative approach to poverty reduction by country officials and the Bank; analyze country policies, public expenditures, and institutions; and recommend actions to strengthen the impact of policies and programs on poverty reduction. In turn, the Bank's country assistance strategies build on the prescriptions for poverty reduction contained in the assessments. The assessments summarize key social indicators such as child mortality, nutrition, immunization, maternal mortality, and fertility. They also indicate special environmental constraints and risks facing the poor. So far, twenty assessments have been completed.

The Bank's support for family planning and other programs to help countries reduce population growth rates is an important component of its approach to poverty reduction. As stressed in the "Poverty Reduction Handbook" and in *World Development Report 1992*, high fertility rates are also an important environmental issue. The Bank's approach is twofold: it focuses both on female education and other important determinants of the demand for family planning services and on more available and accessible family planning services. In the past few years lending for population, health, and nutrition activities has increased dramatically—from $305 million in fiscal 1988 to nearly $1 billion in fiscal 1992.

Addressing Global Challenges

The Global Environment Facility (GEF), established in 1990, is jointly implemented by the United Nations Development Programme (UNDP), the United Nations Environment Programme (UNEP), and the World Bank. An agreement on restructuring the GEF so that it may serve as the interim financing mechanism for the Biodiversity and Climate Change conventions was reached by GEF participants in April 1992 and was endorsed by UNCED. As a result, the GEF is likely to play an increasingly important role in combating global environmental problems—climate change, ozone depletion, loss of biodiversity, and pollution of international waters, as well as land degradation and deforestation, insofar as they relate to these four focal areas.

During fiscal 1992 six GEF investment projects totaling $80 million were approved. These support conservation of the environment in Bhutan; preservation of biodiversity in Mexico and in Poland; replacement of fossil fuels with biomass for energy production in Mauritius; handling and disposal of ships' wastes in six Chinese ports; and afforestation in Ecuador. By June 1992 the Facility was considering more than seventy projects amounting to $580 million.

A breakdown of the portfolio shows that 40 percent of the resources allocated so far are for projects in Asia, 23 percent in Latin America and the Caribbean, 19 percent in the Middle East and North Africa and Eastern Europe regions, 14 percent in Africa, and 4 percent for global and interregional projects. As additional projects are prepared for the rest of the pilot phase, the Bank and its partners—the UNDP and the UNEP—are making a considerable effort to bring more global-warming and African projects into the portfolio.

Future Directions

The Bank has made progress in integrating environmental concerns into its activities through a variety of initiatives ranging from environmental assessment to assisting borrowing countries in the preparation of environmental action plans. But major tasks lie ahead. One such task is the development of practical analytical approaches to help borrowing countries plan and implement strategies and programs for sustainable development. To this end the Bank's expanding research in environmental economics has begun to develop the necessary methodologies for sound environmental management through a comprehensive analysis of the environmental costs and benefits of country economic policies. New initiatives are also under way to improve environmental indicators, which are essential for combining environmental and economic information in policy development, by building on work begun for *World Development Report 1992*. In addition, the Bank is closely involved in efforts to develop a coordinated interagency strategy to implement the provisions of Agenda 21.

The Bank must also move vigorously to implement its environment-related operational directives and incorporate into its work the findings, conclusions, and lessons from its evaluations, assessments, and independent reviews. This will entail increased support for environmental projects, particularly clean water, sanitation, and energy efficiency; improvement of in-house capabilities and technical skills; and more explicit integration of environmental costs and benefits into the economic evaluation of Bank-supported projects and policies.

Individual lending operations and studies will, of course, continue to be important vehicles for the Bank's efforts to help countries address environmental problems. But the environment must assume an important place in the Bank's country dialogue on policies, public expenditures, and institutions. Preparation of environmental action plans is an important step in assessing priorities, formulating policies, and building commitment, but adequate follow-through is also essential to ensure that the priorities identified and the approaches and policies developed are successfully financed and implemented.

The association of the Bank with the operational phase of the Global Environment Facility necessitates closer linkages between global environmental considerations and Bank lending, particularly in the areas of energy planning and development and forest management and agriculture. This calls for more emphasis on country strategies and action plans and for the careful assessment of the global benefits and associated incremental costs of local actions stemming from national development strategies and priorities.

Organization of the Report

The report begins with a discussion, in chapter 1, of the emerging global consensus on the relationship between environment and development and its implications for the Bank's work. Chapter 2 reviews key operational initiatives by the Bank in fiscal 1992, and chapter 3 describes the work of the Global Environment Facility.

Chapter 4 discusses in detail current environmental work in each of the Bank's six geographic regions—Africa, East Asia and the Pacific, South Asia, Europe and Central Asia, the Middle East and North Africa, and Latin America and the Caribbean. A new feature in this year's review of regional environmental operations is a discussion of strategic priorities and new initiatives.

Chapter 5 deals with new and continuing environmental research and policy work, grouped by the main sectors. Coordination between the World Bank and the international community on environmental concerns is outlined in chapter 6. This year's annexes contain not only a list of projects with environmental objectives or components, as in past years, but also a separate list of efforts funded by the GEF.

Notes

1. The World Bank, as defined in this report, includes the International Bank for Reconstruction and Development (IBRD) and its affiliate, the International Development Association (IDA). Other affiliates of IBRD are the International Finance Corporation (IFC) and the Multilateral Investment Guarantee Agency (MIGA). The World Bank, the IFC, and MIGA are sometimes referred to as the World Bank Group.

2. Throughout the report, dollar amounts refer to current U.S. dollars unless otherwise specified. A billion is a thousand million.

1. Integrating Environment and Development

The United Nations Conference on Environment and Development (UNCED), held in Rio de Janeiro in June 1992, brought together heads of state or government from 120 nations and delegations from 178 countries. The Earth Summit was an event unprecedented in size, scope and expectations. Although some were disappointed at the lack of specific commitments to expand aid programs and to set schedules for action, the conference marked a historic endorsement by world leaders of the urgent need for policymakers and planners to view environmental and development policies as mutually reinforcing, not mutually exclusive. The accords that were adopted also demonstrated a remarkable consensus as to the policies and practices needed to achieve environmentally responsible development (box 1-1).

Agenda 21—UNCED's blueprint for environmental action—gives high priority to the implementation of "win-win" policies that exploit the complementarity between poverty reduction, economic efficiency, and sound environmental management. It also notes that unregulated economic growth can have profound and sometimes irreversible effects on the environment. These negative impacts need to be addressed by well-targeted policies, strengthened environmental institutions, and increased allocation of funds for investment in environmental technologies. Hence, any strategy that aims at sustainable management of the earth's resources must both build on the positive links between development and the environment and seek to break the negative links between economic growth and environmental deterioration. Both components are essential. *World Development Report 1992* contains a detailed exposition of these two sets of policies.

Key Elements of the Emerging Consensus

Although it is difficult to give an operationally precise definition of sustainable development, a strong and growing consensus has emerged

Box 1-1. The Earth Summit Accords

- *The Rio Declaration on Environment and Development* sisting of twenty-seven basic principles designed to gᵢ international policies, acknowledges that poor countrie development" and that rich countries bear a special respc of the pressures their societies place on the global environment." The principles cover a broad range of issues, including the link between environment and development, the sovereign right of states to exploit their own resources (without damage to others), international cooperation in eradicating poverty, the role of women in sustainable development, and the use of economic instruments in environmental and development policy.

- *Agenda 21*, the main operational product of UNCED, offers a voluminous blueprint for future environmental action and covers all the main sustainable development issues discussed at the Summit. The Agenda addresses more than 100 program areas, including climate change, marine pollution, deforestation, desertification, human resources, and sustainable agriculture. The Agenda aims at integrating environment and development. It will be supported by new and additional financial resources, improved access to environmentally sound technologies, and strengthened institutional capacity in developing countries. States were called on to prepare sustainable development plans outlining their own environmental problems, as well as their strategies, programs, and priorities for implementing Agenda 21. UNCED agreed that financing should be assembled to support these programs through a variety of existing funding mechanisms: the multilateral development banks, including regional development banks; IDA; the Global Environment Facility; bilateral assistance programs, including debt relief; and voluntary contributions through NGOs, which currently administer about 10 percent of total official development assistance.

Agenda 21 also calls for innovative financing to generate new public and private flows through, among other measures, greater use of debt swaps, economic and fiscal incentives, and reallocation of military resources to development. Existing aid consortia, consultative groups, and roundtables were asked to support these country-based programs by integrating environmental and development assistance strategies and by adjusting their membership and operations to facilitate this process. In addition, UNCED agreed to request the General Assembly of the United Nations, at its next session in September 1992, to establish an intergovernmental committee to negotiate an international convention to combat desertification, particularly in Africa. Finally, a Sustainable Development Commission is to be established under the auspices of the United Nations Economic and Social Council (ECOSOC) to coordinate the results of UNCED.

(Box continues on the following page.)

Box 1-1 (continued)

- *The Climate Change Convention*, signed by 155 countries, aims at stabilizing concentrations of greenhouse gases—carbon dioxide, methane, and other heat-trapping gases, which scientists widely agree may cause global warming. The agreement contains general commitments for all parties with regard to these objectives but sets no specific targets or timetables for emission reductions. Industrial countries are specifically required to adopt policies and measures to limit emissions and "sources" of greenhouse gases and enhance carbon-absorbing "sinks" such as forests. The obligation of developing countries to implement their commitments depends on the financial resources and technology made available to them, taking into account their overriding priorities of economic and social development and poverty reduction.
- *The Convention on Biodiversity* was signed by 157 countries. This convention's main objectives are to protect and sustain the earth's living resources and ecosystems and to share the benefits from the use of genetic resources. Parties to the convention are required to identify important areas of biological diversity; to establish methods of conserving diversity at the site of origin and elsewhere; to regulate access to genetic resources; and to transfer technology relevant to the conservation and sustainable use of biological diversity on mutually agreed terms. The convention calls on industrial countries to provide financial and technical resources to help developing countries conserve their living resources and on investors and developing countries to share equitably the results of biotechnological research and development originating in the developing countries concerned.
- The guiding objective of *Principles for a Global Consensus on Forests* is to reconcile the potential conflicts between the objectives of sound management, conservation, and development of forests. The principles take into account the many functions and uses of forests, including traditional uses, as well as the potential for their development through sustainable forest management. The statement recognizes that poor countries need to use forest products for lumber, food, and fuel, while acknowledging the global value of forests as sources of medicine, as wildlife habitats, and as "sinks" for pollution.

on the directions for policy reform. The following propositions—which will continue to undergird the World Bank's strategy—summarize this consensus.

1. *Poverty reduction is essential.* A central theme of *World Development Report 1992* and Agenda 21 is the strong relationship between poverty reduction and environmental stewardship. Accelerated programs in

primary health care, education, population and family planning, sanitation, water supply, and rural development are central elements of any sustainable development strategy. The allocation of property rights to poor people has a demonstrably positive impact on rural and urban development. Improving the status of women—through better access to education, family planning, health care, and jobs—also yields high environmental returns.

2. *Policies to promote the efficient use of resources benefit both the environment and the economy.* Most governments still subsidize the consumption of certain vital resources. Energy, water, wood, and pesticides, for example, are often inefficiently used because of misplaced government subsidies, and the result is widespread environmental degradation. Other important policies that can yield environmental and efficiency gains include those directed at promoting more open trade and investment (thus facilitating technology transfer and more efficient allocation of resources), improved management of state-owned utilities (to reduce waste and expand the coverage of environmental services), and macroeconomic balance (by developing a longer-term outlook on the part of investors).

3. *Tradeoffs between economic growth and the environment need to be measured and minimized.* Much damage to the biosphere has been brought about by inadequate assessment of potential environmental degradation, underestimation of the costs of environmental damage, and the consequent failure to consider alternative investments. Research and investment are urgently required in three areas: gathering basic data on environmental conditions and trends; evaluating the impacts of economic activity on environment and resources; and identifying alternative means for raising incomes while protecting the environment. Environmental impact assessments help both development institutions and borrowers evaluate the state of resource stocks and identify development options with minimal environmental impacts.

4. *There is a pressing need to strengthen institutional capacity for designing, implementing, and enforcing environmental policies.* Throughout much of the developing world, environmental institutions need to be considerably strengthened if policies for sustainable development are to be successfully planned and implemented. There is an obvious need for capacity building as an integral part of project implementation. Increasingly, institutional inadequacies are proving major obstacles to proper design and implementation of projects. Development assistance institutions therefore need to intensify their efforts to advise on and assist with institutional strengthening so that countries can improve their implementation of environmental policies and better manage key resources.

5. *Additional investments will be required to reduce poverty and protect the environment.* Financing increased investment in developing countries will require higher domestic savings and increased international financial flows. Liberalized trade and investment, debt relief, and increased commercial and official flows all have important roles. IDA and the GEF were identified at UNCED as key channels for increased concessional funding for sustainable development at the national and global levels, respectively. The bulk of the funds for addressing global environmental challenges will have to come from the industrial world. But developing countries must be prepared to utilize investments where they will have the most domestic impact, for the least environmental cost.

The World Bank's Focus on the Environment

In the light of the foregoing considerations, the World Bank's contribution to member countries' efforts to protect and enhance the environment while reducing poverty and developing efficiently has four components.

1. *Assisting member countries in setting priorities, building institutions, and formulating policies for sound environmental stewardship.* The Bank will continue to assist countries in the preparation of national environmental action plans (EAPs) and to provide support for strengthening institutional capacity and financing environmental investments in borrower countries. Such action plans help focus policy and research efforts on critical environmental issues and identify priority areas of investment. In addition, an EAP assists other development institutions and donor agencies in setting targets and priorities for funding. The Bank's country assistance strategies will be reinforced by a strengthened program of analytical and policy work that emphasizes the development of methodologies and best practices relevant to member governments and their pursuit of sustainable development strategies.

2. *Ensuring that Bank lending incorporates environmental concerns at every stage of preparation, design, and implementation.* This will require the Bank to continue to learn from its ongoing experience with environmental assessments and from the experience of other agencies. This year's first annual review of environmental assessments (see chapter 2) and the report of the Independent Review on Narmada will be crucial inputs to the Bank's continuing efforts to strengthen methodology, staffing, and technical assistance to member governments.

3. *Assisting member countries to build on the complementarity between poverty reduction and the environment.* This initiative will require continued efforts to reduce rapid population growth rates; expand poverty reduction programs; enhance the status of women through better edu-

cation and access to health care, family planning, and jobs; provide sanitation facilities and clean water to both rural and urban populations; and design and implement comprehensive rural development strategies that take account of population pressures on key resources, help increase incomes, and emphasize sustainable management of resources.

(4.) *Addressing international environmental challenges through participation in the Global Environment Facility.* The Earth Summit endorsed the GEF as the principal mechanism for assisting developing countries in addressing the global environmental issues of climate change, ozone depletion, loss of biodiversity, and pollution of international waters, as well as land degradation and deforestation insofar as they relate to these four focal areas. The Facility will be expanding its membership and its scope, as GEF participants have agreed to the Facility's restructuring in order that it may act, at least in the interim, as the financing mechanism for the Climate Change and Biodiversity conventions signed in Rio de Janeiro.

2. Key Operational Initiatives

During fiscal 1992 the Bank continued to make progress in integrating environmental considerations into all its activities through a variety of initiatives, including environmental assessments (EAs), environmental action plans (EAPs), and operational directives. The Global Environment Facility, jointly implemented with the UNDP and the UNEP, has continued to evolve as an integral part of the international community's response to global environmental issues.

Improving Environmental Assessment

Notable among this year's achievements is the Operational Directive on Environmental Assessment. The environmental assessment process is central to the integration of environmental concerns into projects supported by the Bank. The new operational directive sets out Bank policy and procedures for assessing lending operations and related types of environmental analysis.

On the basis of accumulated experience, the directive revises and updates the October 1989 operational directive on environmental policy. Early in the project cycle, prior to appraisal, Bank task managers are instructed to review project options to ensure that all environmental consequences are recognized and taken into account in project selection, siting, planning, and design. EAs identify ways of improving projects environmentally by preventing, minimizing, mitigating, or compensating for adverse impacts. Like economic, financial, institutional, and engineering analyses, environmental assessment is an essential part of project preparation and is therefore the borrower's responsibility. The new operational directive also provides guidance on consultation with and disclosure of information to affected groups and local nongovernmental organizations (NGOs).

The operational directive requires Bank staff to classify projects according to three environmental assessment categories, depending on the type, location, sensitivity, and scale of the proposed project, as well as the nature and magnitude of its potential impacts. A project is assigned to category A if it is likely to have significant adverse impacts that may be sensitive, irreversible, and diverse. Category A projects require a full environmental assessment. Examples include dams and reservoirs, industrial estates, large-scale irrigation and flood control, land clearance, and resettlement. Projects are assigned to category B when their impacts are not likely to be as sensitive, numerous, or diverse as category A impacts. Category B projects undergo environmental analysis but do not require a full environmental assessment. Examples include small-scale agroindustry, aquaculture and mariculture, rural electrification, tourism, watershed management, and rural water supply and sanitation projects. No EA or environmental analysis is required for category C projects—such as family planning, education, health, and nutrition projects—because they are unlikely to have adverse environmental impacts. Projects funded under the GEF and GEF components of Bank projects are subject to this directive.

General environmental information for category A projects is now published quarterly as an annex to the *Monthly Operational Summary* of proposed IBRD and IDA projects. One-page environmental data sheets for all projects are available to the public on request.

Annual Review of Environmental Assessment

After two years of experience with environmental assessments, the Bank has completed its first review of the EA process. By the end of fiscal 1992 about thirty environmental assessment summaries had been presented to the Bank's Board of Executive Directors; of these, twenty summaries and eight full EAs were reviewed and evaluated. Although the review focused on the adequacy of the EA procedure, in the future emphasis will shift to the effectiveness and implementation of EAs.

The main purposes of the review were to assess borrowing countries' capacity to conduct EAs and the Bank's progress in strengthening this capacity; to determine whether sufficient Bank resources have been devoted to EAs; to identify and resolve significant problems in carrying out EAs; to design future EA training programs for borrowers and Bank staff; to carry out a comparative cross-regional analysis of EAs; and to enable the Bank's Environment Department to provide better overall guidance to and share best practices with the operations staff.

Although the Bank's EA procedures were found to be realistic, workable, and instrumental in improving development planning and environmental management, problems remain. The review found that more effort is needed to strengthen borrowers' capacity to conduct effective environmental assessments. Underestimation of the time, money, and expertise required for Bank EA activities led to some quality control problems and overloaded Bank technical staff, primarily because of the unanticipated amount of time devoted to assisting borrowers. The review recommended that key borrowing countries be given high priority for EA training and that progress in building capacity be evaluated in the next annual EA review. Bank resources devoted to EAs should also be bolstered until borrowers' capacities have improved.

Policy and technical guidance provided to Bank staff was generally found to be adequate, and dissemination and training are now the main priorities. Training programs have been well received, but greater efforts are still needed to help Bank task managers assume the responsibilities assigned them by the operational directive. Awareness and understanding of EA requirements among Bank staff are growing rapidly, and there is a strong demand for sector-oriented training in the Bank. Sectoral and regional EA approaches need to be improved to comply with the directive's requirements to address alternatives, mitigation measures (and their implementation and funding), monitoring, and environmental management and to provide a better link between country economic planning and the EA process.

The review recommends further training to enable Bank staff to move beyond the generalities of the operational directive and guidelines and concentrate on specific issues and sectors. To improve awareness and understanding of EA requirements, more work should be done to strengthen instructions for sectoral and regional EAs. The project-screening process needs fine-tuning to ensure consistent project categorization and efficient use of Bank resources. Finally, the review suggests that the Bank establish and support project supervision systems in order to strengthen EA implementation and monitoring of approved projects.

Environmental Assessment Sourcebook

The *Environmental Assessment Sourcebook* provides comprehensive EA guidance in the form of a handbook (World Bank 1991a). The first volume, *Policies, Procedures, and Cross-Sectoral Issues*, was published in July 1991. It provides specific advice on social issues, economic analysis, strengthening of local environmental management capabilities and institutions, financial intermediary loans, and, most important, community involvement and the role of NGOs. The other two volumes, also published in fiscal 1992, deal with critical issues in the agriculture, transport, urban infrastructure, energy, and industry sectors.

Training

EA training activities have already been carried out both within the Bank and in borrowing countries. Some have concentrated on implementation of various operational directives, using the *Sourcebook* and examining case studies. Regional Environment Divisions have also organized seminars for staff, and some have commenced in-country training programs. Seven internal courses on environmental assessment were conducted in 1990 and eight in 1991. In 1992 one course was held to review major changes in the revised environmental assessment directive.

Environmental Action Plans

Environmental action plans provide a basis for Bank dialogue with governments on critical environmental issues. Donor support for the preparation of an EAP is provided in response to a country's request. It starts with a complete review of environmental issues to determine national priorities. These priorities are then addressed through a series of policy actions, investment proposals, and institutional changes. The preparation of EAPs involves a broad process of popular participation, organized through various levels of government, including local authorities, and through civic groups, research and academic institutions, NGOs, and other private sector organizations. The new Operational Directive on Environmental Action Plans provides guidance to Bank staff for assisting borrowers in preparing EAPs.

Although each action plan is unique, common goals include (a) furthering environmental policy and legislation; (b) strengthening the institutional framework for dealing with environmental issues; (c) building national capacity for environmental management; (d) establishing environmental monitoring and information systems; (e) developing human resources; and (f) addressing key natural resource management issues in such areas as soils, water, forests, fisheries, and energy.

Responsibility for the preparation and implementation of an EAP rests with the government concerned. The Bank's role is primarily to provide advice and to help arrange technical assistance if requested by the government. The degree of Bank involvement depends on the capacity of the government to design and manage the process; Bank support may be substantial in some countries and minimal in others. Working with each government to promote the integration of an EAP into the government's sectoral and national development plans, the Bank incorporates information from the EAP into its own country assistance strategy and economic and sector work. An environmental action plan is expected to be part of a continuing process whereby the government plans and implements environmental management and to form an integral part of national development policymaking and decisionmaking.

Environmental action plans facilitate donor coordination at the country level by specifying environmental priorities, and they help mobilize appropriate resources and manpower to tackle the problems. To date, seven EAPs have been completed—by Burkina Faso, the Arab Republic of Egypt, Ghana, Lesotho, Madagascar, Rwanda, and Sri Lanka.

Other Environment-Related Operational Directives

The new Operational Directive on Agricultural Pest Management codifies Bank policy for addressing pest management issues in investment lending for the agricultural sector. The Bank advocates the diversified and sustainable approach of integrated pest management (IPM), which involves (a) managing pests rather than seeking to eradicate them; (b) relying as much as possible on nonchemical methods to keep pest populations low; and (c) selecting and applying pesticides, when they have to be used, in a way that minimizes adverse effects on people, on beneficial organisms, and on the environment.

Also issued this fiscal year were the Operational Directive on Indigenous Peoples, which provides more specific guidelines for preventing or mitigating adverse impacts of Bank development projects on indigenous peoples, and the Operational Directive on Poverty Reduction, which provides practical guidelines for implementing the Bank's poverty reduction strategy.

In addition, the Bank's umbrella environmental policy is being revised and updated as an operational directive on environmental policies. This directive will bring together the current thinking of the Bank in order to provide a conceptual basis for all the Bank's work—not only the lending program but also research, country and economic sector work, and international cooperation. The operational directive will emphasize the important links between economic development and environmental concerns.

3. The Global Environment Facility

The Global Environment Facility (GEF) was established in 1990 as a three-year pilot program to provide grants for investment projects, technical assistance, and—to a lesser extent—research. GEF resources are to be used for exploring ways of assisting developing countries to protect the global environment and for transferring environmentally benign technologies. Its activities are therefore intended to be in harmony with the development goals of the countries involved.

The pilot facility assists developing countries in the demonstration of solutions to four main global environmental problems: (a) global warming, particularly the effects on the world's climate of greenhouse gas emissions resulting from the use of fossil fuels and the destruction of carbon-absorbing forests; (b) pollution of international waters through, for example, oil spills and the accumulation of wastes in oceans and international river systems; (c) destruction of biological diversity through the degradation of natural habitats and the "mining" of natural resources; and (d) the depletion of the stratospheric ozone layer caused by emissions of chlorofluorocarbons (CFCs), halons, and other gases.

Responsibility for implementing the GEF is shared by the UNDP, the UNEP, and the World Bank. The Facility was set up with the understanding that no new bureaucracy would be created and that only modest institutional adjustments would be needed in each of the three implementing agencies. Within this tripartite structure, the agencies play distinct roles.

- The UNDP is responsible for technical assistance, capacity building, and project preparation. Through its worldwide network of offices, it helps to identify projects by means of preinvestment studies. It is also charged with running the small-grants program for NGOs.
- The UNEP provides the secretariat for the Scientific and Technical Advisory Panel (described below), as well as environmental expertise and advice on specific projects. It plays a central role in strategic

planning and ensures that the policy framework for the GEF is consistent with conventions and related legal instruments and agreements.

- The World Bank administers the GEF, acts as the repository of the Trust Fund, and is responsible for implementing investment projects.

Projects that benefit the global environment, as distinct from the local environment, qualify for funding under the GEF. To this end, projects must fall into one of the four priority areas described above. But not all projects that benefit the global environment automatically qualify for support from the GEF. Projects financed by the Facility must also be innovative and demonstrate the effectiveness of a particular technology or approach. Given its pilot nature, other criteria include the contribution a project makes to human development (for instance, through education and training) and the provision for evaluation and dissemination of results.

Sixteen eminent scientists from industrial and developing countries serve on the Scientific and Technical Advisory Panel. This independent group has formulated criteria for eligibility and priorities for selection of GEF projects (see Annex C). The panel also reviews project proposals and coordinates research and data collection.

Funding Commitments

The GEF, which has $1.3 billion to commit over the three-year pilot phase that began in 1990, is an umbrella facility made up of funds from three distinct sources. The Global Environment Trust Fund, known as the "core fund," accounts for the bulk of the GEF's resources. In addition, the GEF formally includes several associated cofinancing arrangements. These funds, totaling $300 million, are available on grant or highly concessional terms. Although there are no set rules for allocating Trust Fund resources, in general, 40–50 percent should go to projects to reduce global warming, 30–40 percent to conserve biological diversity, and 10–20 percent to protect international waters. An additional $200 million is allocated separately through the Montreal Protocol's own funding mechanism to combat ozone depletion.[1]

By June 1992 more than $860 million had been pledged to the core fund. Twenty-eight countries (eleven of them in the developing world) had pledged contributions to the GEF: Australia, Austria, Belgium, Brazil, Canada, China, Côte d'Ivoire, Denmark, Egypt, Finland, France, Germany, India, Indonesia, Italy, Japan, Mexico, Morocco, the Netherlands, Nigeria, Norway, Pakistan, Spain, Sweden, Switzerland, Turkey, the

United Kingdom, and the United States. In addition to their contributions to the core fund, Belgium, Japan and Switzerland have separate cofinancing arrangements. Australia has established a cofinancing arrangement, and the United States has set up an arrangement within the U.S. Agency for International Development to finance GEF-type projects. Algeria, Bangladesh, Bhutan, Colombia, Hungary, the Russian Federation, Venezuela, and Zimbabwe are holding discussions with the Facility about possible participation.

Proposals for funding from the Trust Fund can be generated in several ways. Governments, the Bank, the UNDP, and the UNEP, as well as NGOs and the private sector, can all put forward suggestions that meet GEF criteria. All projects must be endorsed by the government of the country in which the project is situated. In most cases governments will submit project ideas directly to the implementing agencies, through the UNDP resident representative, a World Bank field office, the appropriate World Bank regional Environment Division, or the UNEP.

At the end of the fiscal year the GEF portfolio consisted of more than seventy projects amounting to $580 million. Six investment projects totaling $80 million have been approved: environmental conservation in Bhutan; preservation of biodiversity in Mexico and in Poland; replacement of fossil fuels with bagasse for energy production in Mauritius (see box 3-1); handling and disposal of ships' waste in six Chinese ports; and afforestation in Ecuador. The projects in Bhutan and Poland were financed entirely by the GEF. The projects in China, Mauritius, and Mexico were Bank projects in which the GEF funded a component; the Ecuador project was financed by the IFC, and the GEF funded a component.

In attempting to balance the portfolio both thematically and geographically, a determined effort has been made to fill important gaps and utilize experience gained from the pilot phase. As of June 1992, 47 percent of resources from the core fund had been earmarked for biodiversity, 36 percent for global warming, and 17 percent for international waters. Of the total, $379 million is for investment projects implemented by the World Bank; $182 million for technical assistance and $14 million for research, under the auspices of the UNDP; and $9 million for UNEP-sponsored research projects.

Resources allocated thus far break down as follows geographically: 40 percent in Asia, 23 percent in Latin America and the Caribbean, 19 percent in the Middle East and North Africa and in Eastern Europe, 14 percent in Africa, and 4 percent for global and interregional projects. As the agencies prepare projects for the rest of the pilot phase, they are making a considerable effort to bring more global-warming projects into the portfolio and to increase the allocation for Africa.

Box 3-1. Turning Sugarcane Waste into Biomass Energy

Like most islands, Mauritius has limited energy supplies; its hydropower potential is being fully utilized, and this Indian Ocean island must rely increasingly on imported coal or oil to fire its electricity-generating plants. Use of locally produced sugarcane waste as fuel would reduce dependence on imported fossil fuels, which would not only benefit the island's economy but would also reduce carbon dioxide emissions, an important cause of global warming.

Sugarcane production on Mauritius is a major industry, averaging 5.8 million tons a year over the past five years. In processing the sugar, about 1.7 million tons of fibrous waste, or bagasse, are separated from the cane. Nearly 1.5 million tons of bagasse is already used to produce steam for internal use in the sugar mills or to generate electricity for the national grid. But roughly 100,000 tons is burned as waste.

The country's peak energy demand is projected to increase by 100 percent over the next decade, and power plants fired with sugar bagasse or with bagasse and coal offer a low-cost alternative to diesel or wholly coal-fired plants. The potential for increased use of bagasse for electricity production is estimated at about 250,000 tons a year: the 100,000 tons now disposed of as waste, plus another 150,000 tons that could be made available if sugar mills became more efficient in generating and utilizing steam for cane crushing and sugar manufacturing.

The sugar energy project financed by the Bank and the GEF is designed to support the initial phase of the government's Bagasse Energy Development Program. It has three main objectives: (a) to expand bagasse-generated electricity production over a four-to-five-year period from 70 gigawatt hours (GWh) to 110 GWh a year, thus replacing 10,000 tons of diesel fuel with biomass fuel; (b) to promote the efficient use of biomass fuels for energy production through a program of trials and experiments on bagasse transport and utilization of cane tops and other waste materials; and (c) to establish an institutional and organizational framework that can facilitate the implementation of the program and promote donor support for biomass fuels.

According to Bank estimates, replacing diesel oil with biomass fuel will reduce carbon dioxide emissions by about 40,000 tons a year. It will also reduce emissions of heavy metals, reactive hydrocarbons, and other particulates, thus improving the island's air quality.

Beginning in March 1992 a quarterly report on GEF activities is being included in the *Monthly Operational Summary* of proposed IBRD and IDA projects. The report includes details on all GEF investment projects under consideration.

Beyond the Pilot Phase

The pilot phase of the GEF comes to an end in late 1993, by which time all funds will be committed, although actual disbursements are likely to continue until 1997 or 1998. In April 1992 the participating governments reached agreement on the restructuring and future evolution of the GEF. The agreed document, "The GEF: Beyond the Pilot Phase," spells out a set of guiding principles that include the availability of the GEF to serve as the funding mechanism for agreed global environmental conventions. The Facility will finance activities that benefit the global environment within its four focal areas. Land degradation issues, such as desertification and afforestation, as they relate to the four focal areas, will be covered. The participating governments saw universal membership of the GEF as crucial to the Facility's success. The decisionmaking systems in the Participants' Assembly will be designed to ensure an equitable representation of the interests of developing countries while giving due weight to the funding efforts of donor countries. It was also agreed that a single, periodically replenished, funding mechanism has advantages in terms of mobilizing financial resources efficiently and fostering an integrated approach to programming.

Agreement on the restructuring of the GEF was important in forging international consensus on the designation of the GEF as the financial mechanism for the Climate Change and Biodiversity conventions signed at the Earth Summit in Rio de Janeiro, at least until ratification of the conventions. The Summit also supported the efforts for restructuring the GEF and agreed that the GEF was the appropriate financial mechanism to cover the incremental costs of measures outlined in Agenda 21 for the achievement of global environmental benefits. Several countries supported a two- to threefold increase in resources for the GEF once the pilot phase ends in 1993.

Note

1. Countries that have signed the Montreal Protocol on Substances That Deplete the Ozone Layer but are ineligible for funding because their ozone-depleting emissions exceed the limit set by the protocol can receive financing from the GEF.

4. Regional Environmental Operations

Over the past several years the World Bank's environmental lending portfolio has increased considerably, and it is expected to continue expanding in the coming years. Of 222 projects approved by the Bank's Board of Executive Directors during fiscal 1992, 19 were primarily environmental projects (compared with 13 in fiscal 1991), and an additional 43 had significant environmental components (see annex B). The 19 primarily environmental projects represented total Bank lending of nearly $1.2 billion. A project is deemed "primarily" environmental if either the costs of environmental protection measures included in the project or the environmental benefits accruing from the project exceed 50 percent of the project's total costs or benefits. Projects are considered to have "significant environmental components" if environmental protection costs or environmental benefits exceed 10 percent of the total project costs or benefits. Almost 30 percent of all projects approved in fiscal 1992 had significant environmental components.

Six loans (totaling $183.9 million) were approved for major environmental projects in the Africa region in fiscal 1992; an additional eleven projects with significant environmental components were also approved. The Asia and Pacific region had eight environmental projects, amounting to $494.8 million, and sixteen projects with environmental components. The Europe and Central Asia and Middle East and North Africa regions together had six projects with environmental components, and the Latin America and Caribbean region had five major environmental projects, for $498.1 million, and ten projects with environmental components. In addition, six GEF investment projects amounting to nearly $80 million were approved during fiscal 1992 (details are given in chapter 3 and in the sections on individual regions in this chapter).

Africa

The Bank's Africa Region comprises Sub-Saharan Africa and the islands of the Indian Ocean, an area encompassing forty-seven countries with a total population of slightly more than 500 million. Sub-Saharan African countries have the highest rates of population growth in the world, averaging 3 percent a year. At its current rate of growth, for example, Nigeria's population could reach 255 million by 2020, putting severe stress on its resources, infrastructure, and services. The population of Nairobi grew by 600 percent in just two decades (1960–80).

Partly as a consequence of demographic pressure, the region is beset by worsening resource constraints and widespread environmental deterioration: land degradation in the drylands and the humid zones, destruction of tropical forests, and degradation of coastal areas. More than one-third of Sub-Saharan Africa is threatened with recurrent drought. Rapid population growth, inadequate food production and distribution systems, low levels of nutrition, health, and education, and environmental degradation have contributed to increasing poverty, particularly for women and children in rural areas.

Environmental problems are central to the challenge of development facing Africa. The Bank's work in Sub-Saharan Africa is based on helping each country identify and address environmental constraints within its overall development strategy. The number of interested donors and NGOs has grown to such an extent that effective coordination of environmental donors has become an increasingly important and demanding activity for Bank staff.

The regional work program consists of five parts: (a) regional studies to deal with broad areas of concern for environmental management—forestry and dryland management, wildlife, soil conservation, and integrated pest management; (b) country-specific work on national and sectoral strategies for sustainable development, including support for environmental action plans and related country initiatives; (c) lending operations for improved environmental management, including natural resource management, institutional development, and management of urban growth; (d) environmental assessments of Bank operations to ensure participation by the people affected and to ensure that potential impacts are minimized or mitigated; and (e) coordination of the Bank's portfolio of GEF projects in Africa.

Strategic Priorities

The cornerstone of Bank policy toward the environment and development in Africa is the environmental action plan. Today, about half of all Sub-Saharan countries are actively developing such action plans, and many of the others will soon follow. Through the EAP process, local capacities for environmentally sound planning and project implementation are strengthened and broad public participation is brought to bear on decisionmaking concerning development.

THE LENDING PROGRAM. A process for environmental assessment of projects is already well established. Future work will focus more on the supervision and monitoring of the environmental assessment process and on the continued development of analytical tools for task managers. An increasing share of the lending program will be for environmental projects that address, in particular, management of natural resources (especially soils, water, and forests; urban water supply and sanitation, and pollution control) and efforts to strengthen policy frameworks and environmental institutions. Health and education projects will increasingly include environmental components. The region will reinforce its environmental efforts through a major emphasis on population programs and increased attention to sustainability issues in agriculture, development of water resources, and mining and energy projects.

The lending program is supported by regional studies. Recently completed work covers agroforestry, environmental information, wildlife management, and integrated pest management. Ongoing work addresses important topics such as soil fertility, management of drylands and forests, environmental education, environmental economics, and sustainable settlement, including land tenure issues.

The GEF will play a significant role in expanding resources for projects addressing biodiversity and climate change, as well as the consequences of land degradation in drylands and tropical forests. With appropriate institutional support, GEF projects could also help improve the management of river basins and of coastal and near-shore waters.

Recently, the World Bank has begun to work more closely with the African Development Bank. Over the next few years the two institutions will build up capacity for environmental assessments and strengthen institutional capacities for sound environmental planning, notably by linking environmental action plans with national long-term perspective studies. The Global Coalition for Africa, in which the Bank plays a leading role, will be another important vehicle for donor coordination in support of country environmental initiatives.

NEW INITIATIVES. The region will establish a task force to develop a regional medium-term strategy for environmental management, taking into account Agenda 21 and other substantive results of the Earth Summit. The task force will focus on improving environmental planning for sustainable development; developing better processes for environmental monitoring; and reinforcing institutional capacities for environmental management.

The Earth Summit supported the GEF's proposals to add to the portfolio deforestation and land degradation issues as they relate to the Facility's four focal areas. The Bank is also prepared to assist African countries to contribute to a draft convention on land degradation. To this end, a workshop was held in Oslo in August 1992, which drew lessons from Bank experience with dryland management in the Sahelian countries. The regional Technical Department is also preparing regional guidelines to supplement the recent Bank policy paper, *The Forest Sector*.

The secretariat of the Global Coalition for Africa is currently drafting an African Charter for Sustainable Development. This initiative would constitute a new partnership between Africa and the donor community, taking into account the concerns voiced and the commitments made at UNCED. The draft is expected to be discussed at the next meeting of the Organization of African Unity (OAU).

Environmental Action Plans

By the end of the 1980s many developing countries and international agencies had come to realize the close relationship between the environmental, economic, and social aspects of development. But in Sub-Saharan Africa the scarcity of reliable data on the state of the environment, the paucity of persons trained in quantitative and qualitative analysis, and weaknesses in institutions and laws often make it difficult to define environmental objectives and translate them into policies and programs. In response to this situation, a number of African countries, in collaboration with the World Bank and other international partners, have initiated EAPs. Certain countries, although not formally working on EAPs, are preparing national conservation strategies or similar exercises which, to varying degrees, meet the content requirement of EAPs. The Africa region will work with governments, whenever Bank support is requested, to broaden and strengthen these initiatives.

To aid countries in the preparation of EAPs, a secretariat has been established in the African Development Bank in Abidjan with support from the World Bank and other donors. The secretariat will draw on the skills of Africans with experience in environmental action plans to provide training and technical assistance to countries that are just starting the process. The Bank is also supporting the EAP process through special programs to develop African capabilities in environmental economics and environmental information systems. In coming years EAPs will be integrated into the preparation of National Long-Term Perspective Studies, which are aimed at promoting the full integration of environmental considerations into country strategies for sustainable development.

A workshop organized by the World Bank in Dublin in December 1990 brought together representatives from seventeen African countries and a number of bilateral and multilateral donors to discuss the EAP process in Africa. The workshop showed that EAP goals can benefit immensely from a regional approach that brings African experts together to share ideas.

This group of donors and Sub-Saharan African countries has come to be known as the Club of Dublin. With support from the Bank and other agencies, the club is promoting the involvement of African experts in environmental strategy and planning by bringing together distinguished thinkers and decisionmakers from African governments, universities, NGOs, and the donor community. Meetings of the club were held in Mauritius in June 1991 and in Uganda in January 1992. The club is also involved in disseminating information to new teams that are initiating EAPs, improving EAP quality in general, and developing human resources. The Bank, the United Nations Sudano-Sahelian Office (UNSO), and the African Development Bank are now jointly sponsoring a team of African experts, based at the African Development Bank in Abidjan, to assist EAP processes in the region. The club works closely with the Global Coalition for Africa.

Preparation of EAPs has proved to be a rich learning experience. Countries can learn from each other if experiences are documented, analyzed, and publicly discussed. The experience so far has also shown that the participatory preparation of EAPs can be slow and demanding. The process raises fundamental issues of coordination among government departments, and in some cases changes in government have further slowed the process. Providing adequate Bank support for the initiation and preparation of EAPs has also placed heavier demands than anticipated on the Bank's technical, managerial, and financial resources.

Twenty-five countries in Africa are currently formulating environmental action plans with support from the UNDP, the UNSO, the World Bank, and other agencies and bilateral donors. Seven EAPs had been completed by the end of fiscal 1992, by five IDA members and two IBRD countries. Lesotho, Madagascar, and Mauritius have approved and begun implementing their EAPs. In Burkina Faso, Ghana, Rwanda, and the Seychelles plans have been completed and approved but not yet implemented. New EAP country processes have been initiated in Benin, the Gambia, Guinea, Togo, and Uganda, and Burundi, Comoros, Congo, Côte d'Ivoire, Djibouti, Gabon, Guinea-Bissau, Kenya, Malawi, Mozambique, Namibia, and Zambia are just beginning the process. Nigeria has completed a framework plan for preparing a state-level environmental action plan.

Economic and Sector Work

The number of countries conducting strategic environmental planning is likely to grow. The Bank plans to assist those countries that have not yet started on EAPs by preparing environmental strategy papers for discussion. An economic report on environmental policy in Malawi, for example, identifies the causes of natural resource degradation, focusing on land, forests, and water, and proposes a three-year plan of action that includes policy reform, sectoral investments, and institutional strengthening. This work provides a basis for future environmental dialogue with the country and is a first step toward an environmental action plan. Country environmental strategy papers are currently in preparation for Cape Verde, Mali, Niger, and Senegal.

In addition to work on country environmental strategies, many sectoral reviews have specifically addressed environmental issues in the agriculture, forestry, mining, and urban sectors. The region's special program in water supply and sanitation helps to improve environmental conditions for poor households in urban and rural areas and is the basis of a strong participatory approach. Strategic work on population issues and on management in the energy sector has made important contributions toward helping African countries address environmental concerns.

ENVIRONMENTAL ECONOMICS. In the course of preparing EAPs, Ghana, Madagascar and Mauritius have begun to estimate the annual cost of environmental degradation. Despite weak data, the exercise has helped decisionmakers form a rough estimate of the cost of policies that harm the environment; estimates vary from 5 to 15 percent of gross national product (GNP).

To address the cost of environmental degradation in Africa more systematically, the Environment Division of the Africa Region (AFTEN) has initiated a special program of support to build up African capacities in environmental economics. The program's objective is to integrate economic analysis into the EAP process. The program has several main elements: a guidebook on environmental economics directed at economists involved in EAP work; funding for international consultant support to EAP teams; training for local economists to build long-term capabilities; short training courses in environmental economics for EAP staff; support for a one-year course in environmental economics at an African university for EAP staff and civil servants; and establishment of an international support network of researchers.

ENVIRONMENTAL INFORMATION SYSTEMS. In most of Africa, data and access to data are inadequate. EAPs have highlighted the need to reorganize existing environmental data, making it more accessible to users; to introduce pilot monitoring and information systems, particularly mapping and Geographic Information Systems (GIS); and to invest substantially in this field to help manage the environment. The use of Geographic Information Systems has already started in some countries.

In early 1990 AFTEN initiated a program for environmental information systems (EIS) in Sub-Saharan Africa. The goal is to help countries create environmental information systems tailored for resource users, planners, and decisionmakers. The program helps countries identify their needs for environmental information and analyze the technical, institutional, legal, and economic factors that prevent them from meeting those needs. It aids them in finding long-term solutions, partly by learning from existing information systems.

Countries that have participated in the EIS program, sharing information among themselves, include Benin, Botswana, Burkina Faso, Côte d'Ivoire, Ghana, Lesotho, Madagascar, Mali, Senegal, Tanzania, Uganda, Zambia, and Zimbabwe. The degree of involvement depends on the interest of the countries and the availability of international funding. Country case studies are now showing how information handling can be improved in some countries, and they will be used to help develop environmental information systems in other areas. National teams coordinate these studies at the country level (see box 4-1). The EIS program's advisory committee has met four times, with participants coming from fifteen African countries. The program is run by a multidonor secretariat within AFTEN, which has produced reports, guideline notes, and a newsletter of EIS activities.

REGIONAL STUDIES. The activities of Africa's regional studies program for fiscal 1992 address different environmental problems but share five common themes. First, each is linked to the environmental concerns expressed in the Bank's Long-Term Perspective Study, *Sub-Saharan Africa: From Crisis to Sustainable Growth*. Second, the studies are designed to have clear operational relevance, contributing to environmentally sound Bank projects and policy advice. Third, they focus on building Africa's capacity to manage the environment sustainably. Fourth, they are designed to strengthen the environment-related skills of Bank staff. Finally, they have a cross-country perspective, addressing issues that are important for many parts of Sub-Saharan Africa. The recently completed study "The Population, Environment, and Agriculture Nexus in Sub-Saharan Africa" (Cleaver and Schreiber 1991) is an example (see box 4-2).

Reflecting the number of environmental action plans that are being prepared, a report brought out by AFTEN in December 1991, "Issues Facing National Environmental Action Plans in Africa," summarizes the

---

Box 4-1. Improving Environmental Information in Uganda

In Uganda the environmental information system (EIS) program has acted as a catalyst for improving the quality of environmental data and information. In conjunction with the environmental action plan process, it has reinforced awareness among high-level government staff of the need for better environmental information.

Using the EIS program as a framework, a project to improve the management of land and natural resources through the development of a Geographic Information System is being carried out in the National Environment Information Center (NEIC). Since the NEIC started operating in September 1990, work has focused on identifying the users of environmental information and understanding their priority needs in relation to natural resource management. A long-term environmental information strategy and a five-year investment program are being prepared.

The demand for environmental information in Uganda was analyzed by means of a questionnaire encompassing five main groups of users— at the local, urban, district, national, and project levels. The results have shown that certain types of data are prerequisites for the conservation and rational use of the country's resource base: demographic information, agricultural data, and information on energy resources, soils, protected areas, intersectoral problems (for example, climate change), and biological diversity.

In the long term, the NEIC plans to establish and maintain a reliable and up-to-date data base on natural resources and the state of the environment through effective cooperation with the ministries and institutions responsible for information, as well as universities, research institutes, NGOs, and the private sector. It intends to serve as the hub for an entire network of environmental data bases, thereby ensuring data compatibility and the efficient exchange of information, and to carry out data modeling and analysis. It further proposes to maintain a modern reference library and document important findings related to environmental issues. A retrieval service will be set up, and information will be disseminated as widely as possible.

The NEIC plans to actively support national programs promoting an integrated approach to environmental management. It will be a national focal point for the exchange of environmental data with neighboring countries, the UNEP's Global Resource Information Database (GRID), and other international data bases. Finally, it will promote training in environmental data-handling technologies such as Geographic Information Systems and remote sensing.

---

experiences of several countries in the fields of environmental education, environmental information systems, institutional frameworks for environmental management, and the application of environmental econom-

---

Box 4-2. The Africa Nexus Study: The Role of Women in Managing Natural Resources

Sub-Saharan Africa's demographic, agricultural, and environmental problems are closely linked. Key elements of this "nexus" are found in traditional crop production and livestock husbandry methods, land tenure systems and land use practices, the responsibilities of women for rural food production and household maintenance, and traditional methods of utilizing dryland and forest resources. These systems and practices have been increasingly strained over the past three decades, largely because of a rapid acceleration of population growth that began when mortality rates declined in the 1950s while birthrates remained high.

Traditional land use and forest exploitation practices have become direct causes of environmental degradation and resource depletion. Despite considerable investment in new technologies, crop yields—especially of food crops—have stagnated or declined in many countries. Slow agricultural growth, which contributes to slow economic growth, has also impeded a demographic transition from high to low birthrates in many countries. Rapidly expanding poor rural populations increasingly degrade and mine natural resources to ensure day-to-day survival. Furthermore, continuing rapid population growth ties up scarce resources in order to meet current survival and consumption needs—resources that could otherwise be used to create the base for less resource-intensive and more sustainable development.

---

ics to national action plans. It also addresses the issues of funding and accountability through monitoring and evaluation of the EAP process.

On a related theme, a study on environmental information is examining the need for demand-driven and cost-effective environmental data systems. Country case studies are now under way in Madagascar and Uganda. Representatives from ten countries have participated in the meetings of an International Advisory Committee, and a multidonor secretariat has been established to support this network within the Bank. Several reports and a newsletter have been widely circulated, and an in-house data system that provides access to key environmental variables for Africa has been established.

The Sahelian Operational Review continues to draw on the best practices in dryland management for the benefit of countries in the Sahelian region. One important emerging theme is the natural resource management (NRM) approach. The NRM approach is community based, participatory, and holistic. Its main instrument is the village land management plan, which communities design with the help of a multidisciplinary

Many other factors have had a detrimental impact on agriculture and the environment in Africa. These include poor rural infrastructure, lack of private investment in agricultural marketing and processing, and ineffective agricultural support services. The inappropriate price, exchange rate, and fiscal policies pursued by many governments in the region have reduced the profitability and increased the risks of market-oriented agriculture, prevented significant gains in agricultural productivity, and contributed to the persistence of rural poverty. A necessary condition for overcoming the problems of agricultural stagnation and environmental degradation will be to introduce widespread policy reforms, particularly as regards women.

Among the study's conclusions are arguments for easing women's time constraints and improving their productivity by launching initiatives in research, infrastructural development, rural technology, and education. Much can be learned about natural resource management from the experience of local and international NGOs, particularly in establishing rural water supply systems managed by women's groups, developing and popularizing locally appropriate, fuel-efficient stoves, providing improved farming and crop-processing techniques and tools to women, facilitating women's access to land and credit, and improving village-level transport systems. The study contends that such initiatives should be pursued through projects that deal with agricultural research and extension, rural water supply and transport, and credit and land tenure and through education and training which more effectively reach women.

team of technicians. Community "ownership," or acceptance, of the plan is crucial, since implementation is the community's responsibility. The plan includes land use rules that govern access to and exploitation of common assets such as rangeland, forests, and water, and it controls specific land improvements on communal, as well as individually owned, land. The NRM approach has been tested in Burkina Faso, Kenya, Mali, and Senegal. An AFTEN working paper, "Dryland Management in Sub-Saharan Africa: The Search for Sustainable Development Options" (Lusigi and Nekby 1991), was issued in November 1991.

A major study on environment and settlement in Sub-Saharan Africa initiated a review of involuntary resettlement programs in Bank-financed projects in Africa. The goal of the study is to improve Bank practice and develop guidelines for policy discussions with governments. In October 1991 a conference on environment and settlement issues in Africa was held in Uganda, in cooperation with the Institute of Social Research at Makerere University. This conference brought together African policymakers, academic researchers, and development specialists to share experiences and discuss future policy directions. Papers presented at this conference will be published in the coming year.

Research now being conducted on the economics of wildlife management will provide data that can guide future Bank projects, as well as policy advice on wildlife management. The study will analyze the economic potential of integrated wildlife management systems by placing wildlife in an economywide context as a source of income and food and will examine the policy implications of these findings. A case study has been initiated in Zimbabwe, and five more country studies are planned.

Another study examines the special problems of African soils and evaluates technologies for improving and maintaining their fertility under increasingly intensive agricultural use. This research is based on a Bank-hosted workshop, held in January 1992, that was attended by Bank agricultural staff and African and other international experts.

Lending Operations

Of seventy-seven projects in the Africa region presented to the Bank's Board for approval in fiscal 1992, six were free-standing environmental projects that focused primarily on improved environmental management, compared with only three in fiscal 1991. The number will continue to increase in coming years.

ENVIRONMENTAL PROJECTS. The Lobito-Benguela Urban Environmental Rehabilitation Project in Angola, supported by a $45.6 million credit, has three main objectives: to restore water supply and sanitation services in the Lobito-Benguela corridor; to improve living conditions in squatter settlements; and to strengthen institutions responsible for urban services and environmental management and planning. The project will rehabilitate the water supply, sanitation, storm drainage, and solid waste disposal systems in urban areas and will provide clean water, latrines, sanitation, and environmental education. It also calls for replanting trees in the unplanned settlements in the corridor. Project preparation included an environmental analysis of the corridor and the preparation of an environmental action plan.

The Natural Resources Management Project in Benin (a $14.1 million credit) will test models for the management by rural communities of renewable natural resources—land, forests, water, and wildlife—with support from decentralized government services and NGOs. It also provides for the development of national capacity for resource management by strengthening the legislative framework and improving national environmental information systems. The project pays particular attention to issues of land tenure and watershed management.

The main objectives of the Kenya Protected Areas and Wildlife Services Project (a $60.5 million loan) are to halt the decline of the country's wildlife, bolster the system of national parks and protected areas, and develop a sound foundation for an environmentally sustainable wildlife-based tourism industry. The project includes rehabilitating park and reserve infrastructure, strengthening the Kenya Wildlife Service's planning and research capabilities, expanding wildlife education, maintaining a Wildlife Protection Unit to control poaching, and establishing a community wildlife program.

To help reverse widespread degradation of natural resources, the Mali Natural Resource Management Project (a $20.4 million credit) will introduce a rational land use system to strengthen the capacity of local communities to manage their natural resource stocks; bolster the management capacity of the Ministry of Agriculture, Livestock, and the Environment; and support the development of a national environmental information system and a national strategy for management of natural resources.

The aims of the Nigeria Environmental Management Project (a $25 million credit) are to strengthen Nigerian environmental organizations, to establish a program of environmental data collection, and to complete a series of sector studies recommended as a result of the Western Africa Department's fiscal 1991 report, "Towards the Development of an Environmental Action Plan for Nigeria." Under the project, support is provided to the Federal Environmental Protection Agency, the Natural Resources Coordinating Council, the Ecological Fund, federal ministries, and state environmental agencies to plan and implement environmental policy and to monitor and enforce environmental management systems.

The Tanzania Forest Resources Management Project (a $18.3 million credit) supports the implementation of the Tanzania Tropical Forestry Action Plan by strengthening institutions and supporting activities designed to improve the management of forests and land resources. Its programs include the development of a national resource information system, national land policies and programs, and regional forest management plans, as well as village-level woodland management and afforestation projects to be implemented by private organizations and local community groups.

PROJECTS WITH ENVIRONMENTAL COMPONENTS. The Benin Urban Rehabilitation and Management Project supports government infrastructure rehabilitation and environmental sanitation in the country's two largest cities. An environmental study for the Cotonou metropolitan area was carried out during preparation to provide an overall framework for spatial planning and site-specific environmental impact studies.

In Mali a component of the Mining Sector Capacity Building Project will help the government develop environmental, health, and safety regulations for mining, set standards, and train officials to monitor compliance.

A $15 million loan for the Mauritius Sugar Energy Development Project supports the government's Bagasse Energy Development Program. It will finance construction of a bagasse-and-coal-fired power plant; efficiency improvements in sugar processing; training; and institutional support for the program. In connection with this project, two studies will be carried out with $3.3 million of GEF support.

Environmental Assessments

Three projects presented to the Board in fiscal 1992 required full environmental assessments—Mauritius Sugar Energy Development, Lesotho Highlands Water, and Malawi Power V. In addition, environmental assessments were carried out as part of the environmental analyses conducted for Ghana National Feeder Roads Rehabilitation and Maintenance, Mali Natural Resource Management, Mauritania Water Supply, Mozambique Agriculture Services Rehabilitation, Nigeria National Fadama Development, Nigeria State Roads, Nigeria State Water I, and Tanzania Forest Resources Management.

Several engineering and technical assistance credits extended during the year will finance environmental studies for projects in preparation. These credits include: Togo-Benin Engineering; Angola Infrastructure Rehabilitation Engineering; Kenya Mombasa Water Supply Engineering; Lesotho Infrastructure Engineering; Tanzania Engineering; and Zaire SNEL (Société Nationale d'Electricité) Technical Assistance.

Projects under the Global Environment Facility

GEF projects slated for approval total $49 million. The Mauritius Sugar Bio-Energy Technology Project ($3.3 million) has already been approved. Other projects under preparation include Congo Wildlife Protection ($10 million), Kenya Tana River Primates ($6.2 million), and Uganda Conservation of Biological Diversity in the Bwindi Impenetrable Forest and Mgahinga National Park ($4 million). The Congo project will help the government strengthen the management of existing biodiversity reserves and carry out studies leading to the preparation of management plans for additional reserves. The Kenya grant will help establish effective management of a small lowland riverine forest reserve that represents the remaining habitat for two endangered primate species. The GEF project in Uganda will support the preservation of two internationally important biodiversity areas through establishment of a trust fund to be administered by representatives from the government, local and international NGOs, and local communities.

Proposed projects will support conservation of biodiversity through the management and sustainable harvesting of fish resources in Lake Malawi; protection of unique coastal and island ecosystems and control of marine pollution in the Seychelles; management of coastal wetlands in Ghana; expansion of community wildlife management programs in Zimbabwe; and the use of satellite imagery for planning and managing biodiversity projects in Central Africa.

Other GEF project ideas in the initial stage of development include reduction of gas flaring at oil refineries in Nigeria; promotion of wildlife conservation through game ranching at four sites in West Africa; improved management of woodfuels for household use in Mali; planting of hardwood trees in Guinea; development of a park in Mozambique; recycling of urban wastes through a composting program in Uganda; and utilization of biomass energy in Côte d'Ivoire.

Asia and the Pacific

In fiscal 1992 the World Bank split its Asia operations into the East Asia and Pacific region and the South Asia region. The priority environmental issues in each region are reviewed separately. The two regions are treated together in the subsequent discussion of Bank activities in the area.

East Asia and the Pacific

The East Asia and Pacific region consists of nineteen countries and includes much of Southeast Asia, China, and the Pacific islands. It contains about 1.6 billion people—almost a third of the world's population—of which 1.1 billion are in China, the most populous country in the world. Nearly a fifth of the population lives in absolute poverty; most of these poor are in China. The region's population is expected to increase to 2.3 billion by 2025, with most of this growth expected to take place in cities and towns. By 2025 urban areas will contain nearly 63 percent of the total population. There are currently six megacities, with a population of more than 8 million, in East Asia—Shanghai, Seoul, Beijing, Tianjin, Jakarta, and Manila. By the turn of the century Bangkok is expected to join this list.

Several of the countries in the region—China, Indonesia, the Republic of Korea, Malaysia, and Thailand—exhibited robust economic growth during the past decade. Rapid industrialization has been the engine for growth, and industry contributes more than a third of gross domestic product (GDP) in these countries. In the East Asia and Pacific region, however, industrialization without adequate environmental management has led to some of the most polluted air, water, and land in the world. To compound the problem, almost all industrial activity is concentrated in densely populated urban centers. The combined effect of industrial and domestic pollution is causing severe damage to the urban environment and is adversely affecting the health of the population. Since most of the cities in the region are located along the coast, fragile coastal habitats and fisheries are under threat from nonsustainable development and resource degradation.

During the past decade continental and insular Southeast Asia experienced the highest rates of deforestation in the world. Deforestation is now a serious problem in countries such as Cambodia, Lao PDR, and Myanmar, where national control over logging has broken down and resources are being exploited with little regard for long-term economic or environmental considerations. Once-dominant exporters such as the Philippines and Thailand have virtually exhausted their forests. Rapid deforestation, combined with environmentally damaging agricultural practices (primarily in the upland areas), is causing soil erosion, disruption of hydrologic regimes, and loss of biodiversity, especially in Indonesia, the Philippines, Thailand, and parts of Malaysia.

Regionwide and transnational environmental issues include acid rain—particularly in China and Japan—and the increasing pollution of Southeast Asian seas. Regional emissions of greenhouse gases—currently about 20 percent of global emissions—are set to rise to 30 percent of world totals by 2000 unless remedial measures are taken.

South Asia

About half the world's poor live in the seven countries of South Asia, stretching from Afghanistan to Bangladesh. Nearly half the region's 1.1 billion people live in absolute poverty, most of them in India. The population of the region is expected to increase to about 2 billion by 2025, with most of the growth taking place in urban areas. By 2025 more than 50 percent of the population is expected to reside in cities and towns. Currently, the region has three megacities—Calcutta, Bombay, and Delhi. By the turn of the century, three more cities, Dhaka, Karachi and Bangalore, are expected to have more than 8 million people.

Pollution from urban wastes—particularly raw sewage and garbage— is a serious problem in Bangladesh, India, and Pakistan, and industrial pollution is a widespread problem in India. Large sections of the population continue to have no access to safe drinking water and sanitation.

Even where sanitation facilities are available, domestic waste is usually dumped untreated into watercourses, polluting them and making them unfit for further use.

Most of the countries in the region suffer from serious degradation of natural resources. High population density has contributed to deforestation not only because of land clearing for agriculture and settlement but also through overharvesting of forests for fuelwood and fodder. Soil erosion is common in the Himalayas (India and Nepal), where market fragmentation constrains economic diversification. Problems of water scarcity and water quality are widespread and are sometimes exacerbated by unresolved water use conflicts among riparian countries. Desertification is a serious problem in South Asia, affecting nearly 200 million hectares, primarily in Afghanistan, India, and Pakistan. More than a third of irrigated land in India and a quarter in Pakistan are affected by waterlogging and salinity. In India biodiversity is seriously threatened by human encroachment and other weaknesses in the protected area system. In Bangladesh, where only 6 percent of the original habitat is intact, the last of the mangroves in the Sunderbans (the coastal marshes) are declining because of overexploitation for fuelwood, building materials, and fishponds, further reducing the habitat of the Bengal tiger. Degradation of marine and coastal resources is emerging as a serious issue.

Strategic Priorities

The Bank's strategy for strengthening environmental activities in Asia focuses on improving institutional capacities, as part of better policies and increased investments in priority sectors. An important aspect of this work is to fit environmental activities into the broader national policy and planning framework. In the areas of policy and institutions, the Bank's work emphasizes:

- Strengthening the ability of national environmental agencies to create sound environmental policies and set standards
- Reinforcing efforts by government ministries to align pricing and trade policies with the objectives of sustainable development
- Strengthening the ability of national, provincial, and municipal agencies to monitor and enforce environmental regulations
- Assisting government agencies and parastatals (such as power utilities and water and irrigation authorities) in conducting environmental assessments of planned capital projects
- Assisting governments to complete and implement their environmental action plans

• Encouraging broader participation by the public, including local NGOs, in the environmental assessment and environmental action plan processes.

Much more effort is needed in these priority areas. Accordingly, the Bank will continue to assist countries in preparing and implementing environmental action plans and will increase its effort to incorporate environmental analysis into country economic memoranda and country strategy papers.

Investment Priorities

THE URBAN SECTOR. The Bank's urban strategy in the region has three aspects. First, the Bank is promoting a collaborative approach to urban and industrial environmental management, in which a strategic consensus is reached by key government agencies, relevant private sector representatives, and important NGOs and community groups. The Metropolitan Environmental Improvement Project (MEIP) is an example (see box 4-3).

Second, water supply, sanitation, and solid wastes are priority issues that require investments, pricing reform, institutional strengthening, and increased collaboration with NGOs. There is a critical need for proper management of water resources.

Third, new approaches to urban congestion and air pollution are being incorporated into Bank urban projects throughout the region (in Bangladesh, China, India, Indonesia, Korea, Pakistan, Philippines, and Thailand). These innovative approaches include taxes on vehicles, fuels, parking, or road usage; efforts to reduce congestion, including better traffic management and vehicle inspection programs; and programs to upgrade technologies and fuels by, for example, encouraging the use of unleaded gasoline and more fuel-efficient engines.

INDUSTRY AND ENERGY. The Bank is in the initial stages of developing a broadly based industrial pollution control strategy for Asia. Three projects, in China, India, and Indonesia, are part of a "first-generation" effort to design comprehensive projects for controlling industrial pollution. Lessons from these projects will be incorporated into a rapidly expanding lending program. In the energy sector the Bank is emphasizing market-based policy reforms to stimulate supply-side efficiency, demand-side conservation, and modernization of equipment. In addition, the Bank has created a unit for alternative energy in the Asia Technical Department.

Box 4-3. Improving Urban Environments through the Metropolitan Environmental Improvement Program

Asian cities have grown rapidly over the past thirty years, and their growth continues to accelerate. If current trends continue, 60 percent of Asia's projected population of 2.9 billion people will live in towns and cities by 2025—a tripling of the number of urban dwellers in 1985. Rapid urban growth and industrialization have led to pervasive pollution of air, water, and land, undermining the benefits of development and imposing a heavy burden on urban residents, especially the poor.

Governments in Asia are beginning to address these urban problems by investing in sewerage, solid waste disposal, and slum improvement; by establishing environmental standards and developing enforcement mechanisms; and by employing planning and environmental impact assessment procedures to guide urban development. But environmental management capabilities still need to be strengthened in many countries.

The Metropolitan Environmental Improvement Program (MEIP), established in 1989 to assist these efforts, is administered by the World Bank, with basic funding for core programs provided by the UNDP. Its first phase concentrates on five cities: Beijing, Bombay, Colombo, Jakarta and Manila. The MEIP's unique mandate is to combine the planning and monitoring of the more traditional sectoral donor activities in metropolitan areas—in, for example, water supply and sanitation, solid waste management, transport, and industry—and so achieve an integrated view of the impact of these activities on the land, air, and water. To facilitate this, environmental management strategies (EMS) are being prepared in all five cities; most will be completed by early 1993.

Work in each city is guided by a steering committee composed of representatives from the central and local government agencies responsible for economic planning, environmental protection, sectoral development, land use, and urban planning, as well as from the private sector and NGOs. Working groups are formed to oversee the technical aspects of specific projects. The MEIP's practice of working with and bringing together government agencies, NGOs, community groups, and the private sector has earned it widespread support in the participating cities.

To strengthen the capabilities of government agencies, the MEIP helps to bolster their institutional relationships and improve their environmental management capacities. The MEIP is also assisting the five cities in preparing feasibility studies to address high-priority environmental management interventions. These studies are generally components of Bank projects, with follow-up investments intended for subsequent projects. Activities under way in fiscal 1992 include the Beira Lake Restoration

(Box continues on the following page.)

Box 4-3 (continued)

Project in Colombo; industrial pollution control projects (concentrating on wastewater treatment in industrial estates) in Bombay and Colombo; case studies of the management experience of Beijing's environmental institutions over the past fifteen years; feasibility studies for the establishment of hazardous waste disposal facilities in Jakarta and Bombay; a regional air quality management initiative that includes Bombay and Jakarta; and projects in Manila and Colombo to develop new credit arrangements for financing pollution control programs and improving the management of pollution control agencies.

Local efforts supported by the MEIP through NGOs and community groups include on-site waste collection in Bombay; the Clean Settlements Program in Colombo, which works to help low-income communities manage their own environments; composting and recycling in Jakarta; and pilot programs in Metro Manila to expand public sanitation services and upgrade the Balikatan women's movement's resource recovery model.

The MEIP encourages participating cities to share their experiences through intercountry research, workshops, and cooperative efforts. Bombay and Beijing assisted Colombo in establishing an air quality management program. This effort was sparked by the Second Intercountry Workshop, held in Beijing in October 1991.

AGRICULTURE, FORESTRY, AND BIODIVERSITY. Within the agriculture sector there has been a shift in the nature of agricultural development projects. Projects involving soil reclamation, sustainable upland farming, integrated pest management, and mariculture are expected to become increasingly common. Because of continued deforestation, the Bank's future forestry work must concentrate on sustainable forest management, with a renewed emphasis on pricing and trade policies relating to forest products.

REGIONAL AND GLOBAL CONCERNS. Air pollution levels in many Asian countries are rapidly increasing, coastal marine pollution is worsening, and loss of biodiversity continues. To help deal with these problems, the Bank is conducting a regional study of acid rain emissions that is expected to lead to policy interventions and lending designed to reduce acid rain at its source. In addition, a regional inventory of work is being carried out in six countries to facilitate the phaseout of CFCs under the Montreal Protocol Interim Fund. Biodiversity action plans have been initiated in about a dozen countries, and a regional strategy has been prepared.

FUTURE LENDING. Environmental lending in the two Asia regions is expected to be on the order of $1.5 billion a year over the next three years. The lending program will continue to emphasize institutional strengthening in order to foster the design and implementation of sound environmental policies and practices.

Environmental components in urban lending, including water supply, are likely to total $625 million a year during 1993–96—$485 million in East Asia and $140 million in South Asia. Urban environmental projects are planned for China, India, Indonesia, and Pakistan. The Metropolitan Environmental Improvement Program plans to include additional cities during its second phase .

Industrial- and energy-related environmental lending is projected to be $215 million a year between 1993 and 1995, of which $115 million is in East Asia. An environmental assessment of the industrial sector in the Philippines is planned; in Indonesia and the Philippines the state of environmental management will be reviewed to facilitate formulation of a long-term strategy; and in India and Indonesia the energy sector strategy will be reviewed with the aim of addressing the environmental implications of energy development.

Environmental components of lending for agriculture and natural resources are expected to reach $660 million a year during 1993–96, of which $410 million a year is in East Asia and $250 million is in South Asia. Newer approaches in these sectors, particularly with regard to soil conservation and rehabilitation, watershed protection, forest management, and integrated pest management are more evident in East Asia than in South Asia, but this situation is expected to change in the medium term. Bhutan, China, Indonesia, Lao PDR, Nepal, Papua New Guinea, Thailand, and Viet Nam will receive support for conservation and management of forests, soil, and natural resources.

In addition to free-standing environmental projects, a significant number of Bank projects are expected to carry environmental components or provide direct environmental benefits. A regional initiative to link key donors and channel investments to areas of highest priority is under discussion .

Bank Environmental Activities

The Bank has taken significant steps to incorporate environmental concerns into its programs in Asia. As elsewhere, the strategy combines environmental lending, more stringent environmental assessment of projects, and nonproject activities designed to improve the ability of member governments to manage their resources. Nonproject activities include supporting environmental action plans, prioritizing future environmental investments, strengthening local institutions that create and implement environmental policies and regulations, and funding analytical work in key technical areas.

In the past, World Bank involvement in the *industrial* sector concentrated on large, often isolated, single-plant operations that lent themselves to "end-of-the-pipe" pollution abatement (measures applied at the end of the industrial process). Today, 70 percent of industrial lending in the region takes place through financial intermediaries, and most industries are in urban areas. Accordingly, the two Asia regions place increased emphasis on preventing and controlling urban pollution and on working with governments and financial intermediaries to combat industrial pollution (see box 4-4).

Industrial and urban projects make available significant financial resources for solid waste management, water treatment, hazardous waste management, pollution control equipment, and shifts to cleaner technologies. The Bank's experience to date, coupled with that of the Metropolitan Environmental Improvement Program, indicates that pollution abatement and sound environmental management in urban and industrial areas also depend on a broad spectrum of interventions that involve legislation, standards, permits, zoning, enforcement capability, and development of institutional and human resources. These features are expected to be more frequently incorporated in future projects.

In the *energy* sector, nearly 80 percent of all new power-generating capacity installed during the 1990s will be concentrated in the developing world; 80 percent of this will be in Asia. The Bank strategy is designed to ensure that policies and prices take due account of environmental costs and side-effects, that supply-side alternatives have been evaluated with environmental considerations in mind, and that alternative energy and demand-management options are considered. Where coal remains the overwhelming choice for energy generation, the Bank will argue that clean-coal technologies, efficiency considerations, and pricing issues must be fully taken into account.

The Bank's most advanced work in the region's energy sector is being done in China, through the Energy Conservation Study and the GEF-financed analysis of greenhouse gas emissions; in India, through additional GEF-financed analysis of greenhouse gas emissions; and in Thailand, through a demand-side management program. Additional technology-related project work is being conducted in China (the Coal Bed Methane Recovery Project) and India (the Non-Conventional Energy Project).

Water quantity, quality, and allocation issues are pervasive throughout Asia. Water shortages are starting to constrain growth, especially in northern China and southern India. Water quality is declining in almost

Box 4-4. Cleaning up India's Dirty Industries

India has enacted comprehensive pollution control legislation and has introduced tough measures for industry, but only 55 percent of all industrial polluters comply with these regulations. As a result, industrial pollution and the associated environmental degradation of surface water, groundwater, air, and soils continue to be a major concern and an increasing threat to the sustainability of India's economic development.

Mounting industrial pollution and its environmental impacts prompted the initiation of the India Industrial Pollution Control Project, approved in May 1991, to support the government's efforts to prevent and alleviate environmental degradation caused by industrial operations, primarily in the chemical industries. The $155.6 million loan and credit will assist in the identification and implementation of a cost-effective program for industrial pollution monitoring, control, and abatement by:

- Promoting effective and timely enforcement of existing legislation to control industrial pollution
- Supporting efforts by industry to comply with existing environmental regulations, including a special effort designed to reach small-scale industry by setting up common treatment facilities
- Supporting assessments, extension services, and research in waste minimization, resource recovery, and pollution abatement.

The project focuses on major sources of pollution from the chemical and related industries, including fertilizers, leather tanning, dyes, pesticides, pharmaceuticals, petrochemicals, pulp and paper, sugar, and distilleries. The four states targeted for the cleanup effort—Gujarat, Maharashtra, Tamil Nadu, and Uttar Pradesh—are centers for the bulk of India's chemical and related industrial sectors. Uttar Pradesh, the largest and most urbanized of the four, has a large number of small and medium-size industrial plants.

The project has three main components:

- *The institutional component* will strengthen the government's monitoring and enforcement ability by financing a program of improvements at the Central and selected State Pollution Control Boards. This component finances a technical and managerial training program, analytical and monitoring equipment needed to upgrade the technical capabilities of the boards, and other laboratory facilities, including mobile monitoring stations.
- *The investment component* will finance individual projects in the target sectors dealing with waste minimization, resource recovery, and pollution abatement; the establishment of common treatment facilities at industrial estates for the treatment of liquid and solid wastes;

(Box continues on the following page.)

all urban and rural settings, creating serious health risks. Furthermore, competition for water is increasing among users—not only among farmers but also between agricultural and urban uses and between countries that share rivers (for example India and Pakistan, India and Bangladesh, and the countries that draw on the Mekong River).

Proposed water resource projects in the Asia region are of a scale and complexity only rarely seen in the past. In agriculture, water issues are highlighting difficult production and institutional issues related to water use and pricing and the rehabilitation of salinized and waterlogged soils. In cities and industries, water resource policies, including pricing and regulation, are bringing about new institutional and participatory approaches to the enforcement of standards and the resolution of disputes. Pollution of surface water, overexploitation of groundwater, and salinization of aquifers are increasing the need for large interbasin transfers to bring water to regions of scarcity. These projects, which are under active consideration in China, India, and Thailand, are hugely expensive and have their own difficult environmental repercussions. All these issues may combine to make water supply the major crisis of the next century for Asia.

Economic and Sector Work

Two regionwide studies were completed in the past year. The Asian Forestry Development strategy advocates different approaches for forest-surplus and forest-deficit countries (that is, countries that use less, or more, wood than they produce). In surplus countries—Fiji, Indonesia, Lao PDR, Malaysia, Myanmar, Papua New Guinea, and the Solomon Islands—the Bank will attempt to press for the designation of areas that are large enough to safeguard critical habitats and biodiversity and protect watersheds and forest dwellers. In forest-deficit countries Bank assistance will be geared toward supporting forest management institutions and making the necessary information available, assisting with strategic planning, revising incentives and other factors that hamper private initiative, and encouraging popular participation in forest management and conservation. The strategy emphasizes the importance of policy, training, participation, and data gathering in future forestry projects.

The Asia Population Issues Paper documents the effectiveness of family planning programs and argues for expanded investment both in family planning and in social and educational services for women. It shows, however, that regardless of the level of services provided, a substantial increase (70–80 percent) in Asia's population over the next forty years is unavoidable because of the region's relatively youthful demographic profile. It projects that Asia's rural population will peak at about 2.1 billion in 2005 and will fall to 1.98 billion by 2025, implying a scale and speed of urbanization that will place enormous pressures on what are still sparse and unreliable basic infrastructure and services.

Asiawide background papers are being prepared on biodiversity, atmospheric emissions, the environmental implications of power generation, industrial pollution, the urban environment, population, institutional strengthening, and natural resource management. They will be completed in fiscal 1993 and will be incorporated into an Asia Environment Report.

Lending Operations

ENVIRONMENTAL PROJECTS. A credit of $49.6 million was approved for the Forest Resources Management Project in Bangladesh. One of the government's objectives is to optimize sustainable production from existing, but limited, forestlands. This project is designed to achieve the development and conservation goals outlined in the Bank's forest sector policy paper. It will establish and maintain a forest management system to attain sustainable development and protect the country's environment and will support popular participation in forest development.

Three environmental projects in China were approved. An IDA credit of $100 million supports the Tianjin Urban Development and Environment Project, the first Bank project to improve the infrastructure and environment in Tianjin, China's third largest city. The project will support long-term urban infrastructure improvements by assisting the municipal government to increase the efficiency and effectiveness of the city's environmental management systems and will help to finance high-priority, long-term investments such as improved drainage, sewerage, solid waste disposal, traffic management, and public transport.

A $125 million Bank loan and credit for the Beijing Environmental Project will assist the city in planning cost-effective strategies for a comprehensive environmental protection program, strengthen the policy and institutional framework required, and support priority investments needed to start the process. The project will address pollution problems associated with air and water quality and with the disposal of domestic and industrial solid wastes.

The Ship Waste Disposal Project, assisted by an IDA credit of $15 million and additional GEF financing of $30 million, will help China reduce pollution of international waters caused by oily wastes and bilge slops from ships. It calls for improved monitoring and analysis of the nature and magnitude of the problem; improved policy, regulatory, and incentive frameworks; and the provision of facilities to receive, process, and dispose of ships' wastes.

A $12 million loan for the BAPEDAL Development Technical Assistance Project in Indonesia will assist with the implementation of the Five-Year Development Plan for BAPEDAL, a new environmental protection agency. The plan will strengthen the institutional capacity and role of BAPEDAL and other agencies responsible for environmental management and pollution control and will design and implement pollution control measures at the national and regional levels.

Korea's Pusan and Taejon Sewerage Project, assisted by a Bank loan of $40 million, will support the 1990–96 National Wastewater Treatment Plan, which is designed to improve water quality in the country's rivers and coastal waters.

A $29.2 million credit for the Environmental Protection and Resource Conservation Project in Pakistan will help the government strengthen institutional capabilities for dealing with environmental problems, implement measures to protect and rehabilitate the environment and conserve natural resources, and provide education and training to create public awareness of the problems and the measures needed to deal with them.

A $124 million credit in support of the Maharashtra Forestry Project in India will help finance integrated investments in the entire forest sector. It will focus particularly on private and public wasteland development, soil and water conservation, wildlife preservation, agroforestry, institutional strengthening, and management of common property and resources.

PROJECTS WITH ENVIRONMENTAL COMPONENTS. Sixteen projects approved in fiscal 1992 had significant environmental components or provided environmental benefits. About 40 percent of these projects were in the agriculture, forestry, and natural resources sector and nearly a third were in the energy sector.

For example, an energy sector loan to Korea would substitute natural gas for high-sulfur-emitting fuels such as coal and heavy fuel oil. In Nepal the Power Sector Efficiency Project addresses both supply-side and demand-side efficiency issues through institution building, training, and industrial energy audits, in combination with physical investments in the infrastructure for distribution. A loan approved for an agriculture project in Papua New Guinea will help protect the world's largest and most endangered butterfly, the Queen Alexandra birdwing.

Environmental Assessment

The integration of environmental concerns into the lending program is not limited to environmental projects and components. Integration is also achieved through the use of the environmental assessment process as a major decisionmaking tool in the project cycle. Of the new projects approved in fiscal 1992, fourteen were classified as A projects, thirty as B projects, and twenty-four as C projects (see chapter 2 for an explanation of the categories).

All told, environmental assessment work is under way in nearly sixty projects. The primary responsibility for the EA falls on the borrowing country government, although the Bank assists in drafting terms of reference for the EAs themselves and works closely with governments in the review and completion of draft EAs. Work still needs to be done to acquaint borrower countries and implementing agencies with Bank guidelines for environmental assessments and for consultation and disclosure of documents. In most cases considerable work is needed to strengthen country capacity to carry out EAs.

Environmental Action Plans

Most countries in the region prepared country reports for UNCED. In conjunction with, and as supplements to, these reports, most countries are also preparing environmental action plans. Sri Lanka has completed the EAP process, and several other countries, including Bangladesh, China, and Pakistan, have completed drafts.

Once an EAP is complete, the Bank turns to follow-up and funding of priority activities identified in the plan. Many donor and nonprofit organizations are involved in this process. The strongest role for the Bank will be in helping translate completed EAPs into viable programs, developing appropriate policy frameworks for determining investment priorities, and, as appropriate, incorporating new investments into its project pipeline.

Apart from the EAPs undertaken by borrower countries, the Bank has undertaken environmental strategy papers in Bangladesh and China and is starting similar work, to be completed in fiscal 1993, in Indonesia, the Philippines, and Thailand. Like EAPs, these papers identify priority environmental issues and—drawing on discussions with borrowing country governments—recommend a detailed action agenda for the future. In China the strategy paper will serve as the basis for the government's expanded environmental work program for the next three to five years.

Projects under the Global Environment Facility and the Montreal Protocol

During fiscal 1992 two Bank-executed GEF projects totaling $40 million were approved. The first establishes a trust fund for biodiversity and conservation efforts in Bhutan, and the second provides for the proper disposal of ships' wastes in China (in conjunction with the Bank project described above). In addition, the UNDP and other agencies approved and began executing five technical assistance and training projects. Three deal with conservation in Nepal, Sri Lanka, and Viet Nam. The other two are in China and support a greenhouse gas study and a pilot project for coal methanation.

Three projects under the Montreal Protocol were appraised during fiscal 1992: in Malaysia, mobile air conditioning systems recycling and Halon control, recovery, and recycling, and in the Philippines and in Thailand, controlled substances engineering projects. The government of the Philippines has given its consent for the project to begin, and agreements are expected to be signed soon with the other two governments. In China a project for phasing out ozone-depleting substances was preappraised, and an agreement is expected to be signed by the government in fiscal 1993. In India a project to reduce ozone-depleting substances is being planned.

Europe and Central Asia

Together, the countries of Central and Eastern Europe and Central Asia—Albania, Bulgaria, the Czech and Slovak Republic, Hungary, Poland, Romania, Yugoslavia, and the fifteen republics of the former U.S.S.R.—have a combined population of about 412 million. In much of Eastern Europe and in the Baltic states, Belarus, the Russian Federation, and Ukraine the population is growing by less than 0.5 percent a year; some countries, such as Bulgaria and Hungary, are experiencing a population decline. In the Central Asian republics, however, growth rates of 3 percent or more are not uncommon.

As diverse as this region is, the countries share similar environmental problems. Many of their problems with pollution are a direct result of past policies that sustained the use of outdated technologies and poor-quality fuels. Throughout the region, central planning has left a legacy of large, inefficient, and highly polluting industries, unsustainable agricultural practices, and mounting pressures on natural resources.

Some of the most severe health problems are caused by toxic emissions or effluents from specific industries such as nonferrous smelters, coking and chemical plants, and steelworks located near communities or cities. Chronic respiratory and related illnesses, however, are often caused by common air pollutants—particulates, sulfur dioxide, and carbon monoxide. Most serious in this regard is the high ambient concentration of particulates in some areas from numerous low-level sources, such as home heating appliances or small industrial boilers that burn coal or oil, and from local "smokestack industries" with insufficient pollution controls. The health impact is magnified in cities with a high concentration of heavy industries that rely on coal for small-scale uses.

Serious health and environmental problems also exist in some areas as a result of specific accidents at nuclear power, fuel-reprocessing, or waste storage plants and surface contamination in nuclear weapons testing grounds. The inadequate design and management of some nuclear facilities and waste sites remain potential hazards.

Although the long-distance transport of pollutants such as sulfur dioxide and nitrogen dioxide—the precursors of acid rain—cause acidification problems across Central and Eastern Europe, from the standpoint of human health local sources of pollution pose the most serious risks. This situation presents a dilemma. The Eastern European countries, along with the Baltic states and the republics of the former U.S.S.R., have expressed interest in harmonizing their policies and standards with those prevailing in Western Europe. Meeting European standards for controlling sulfur dioxide, however, will require expenditure of scarce capital to address a transboundary problem that has far less impact on human health than does localized pollution.

Strategic Priorities

Because the recent political and economic changes have led to significant declines in production and therefore, to some extent, in pollution, some environmental benefits will diminish as the economies of the region

52

recover. Long-term solutions to environmental problems will require fundamental structural changes in the affected economic and management systems and may involve far-reaching social dislocations. Of paramount importance will be policies aimed at better energy pricing, restructuring and modernization of key industries such as mining, metallurgy, chemicals, and petrochemicals, and the creation of new economic activities in areas that have relied primarily on heavy industry in the past. Restructuring and privatization will eventually spur greater economic accountability and more efficient use of natural resources, but such efforts will take time.

Taking the environmental effects of economic reform into account, there is a hierarchy of measures that have the potential for improving environmental conditions in the region. These measures include:

- *Market reform,* associated especially with increases in energy prices
- *Economic and industrial restructuring,* including a steady pace of capital stock turnover, as well as improved approaches to industrial management
- Specific *environmental policies,* meaningful regulations, and credible enforcement backed by well-staffed and innovative institutions
- Targeted *environmental expenditures* in sectors where the other measures are not effective.

Market reform and economic restructuring are proceeding at different rates in different countries. The challenge for environmental policymakers is to phase in regulatory policies and compliance strategies that both complement and encourage structural reforms.

The Bank's sector work to date, with its emphasis on identifying priorities for human health, suggests the need for greater attention to local air pollution, shifting gradually to water pollution and municipal solid waste management as more resources become available and local and regional institutions become established under new political conditions. In rural areas, management of water quality and availability is already a high priority.

There is also a need to reassess energy strategies and identify low-cost approaches that incorporate environmental considerations. Options include improving energy efficiency, identifying a suitable combination of alternatives, and encouraging the development of safe energy sources, such as natural gas, that are available and relatively abundant. This would facilitate dealing with current environmental problems associated with past energy production and consumption patterns.

ENVIRONMENTAL POLICIES. Environmental standards in Central and Eastern Europe are often stricter than in the European Community or the United States. But they are largely unenforced and are in many cases unenforceable. The countries of the region must establish appropriate regulatory mechanisms (using both command and market-based instruments) that are based on politically acceptable revision of excessively strict standards and that reinforce the likely improvements in the capital stock which should result from industrial restructuring.

Environmental expenditures should focus on cost-effective, low-waste technologies that provide widespread benefits and have the potential to be upgraded as additional resources become available. In designing investment approaches (for example, in the power sector), least-cost programs need to be identified for the sector as a whole. Due consideration should be given to intercountry exchanges of power to meet short- and long-term national imbalances of supply and demand. Environmental considerations should be an integral part of this process and might require a mix of measures, such as fuel switching, scheduling, location-specific management practices, and temporary or longer-term rehabilitation.

NEW INITIATIVES. Environment staff in the Europe and Central Asia region and the Middle East and North Africa region are active in facilitating and participating in the formulation of strategic regional environmental action plans, some ongoing and others recently initiated. These include a regional environmental action program for Central and Eastern Europe and an Environmental Program for International Waters, which comprises the Danube, Baltic Sea, Black Sea, and Mediterranean environmental management programs. These programs are described below. (The Mediterranean program is discussed in the section on the Middle East and North Africa.)

The Environmental Action Program for Central and Eastern Europe. The Bank, in cooperation with the OECD, is assisting in the preparation of an environmental action program for Central and Eastern Europe, in response to a request in 1991 by some thirty member governments of the United Nations Economic Commission for Europe (ECE). The program will be submitted to the next Conference of European Environment Ministers in the spring of 1993 and will help establish environmental priorities in a situation of extreme resource scarcity. As part of this exercise, the regional Environment Division is coordinating a study executed in collaboration with the Expert Group on Environment of the ECE and the Commission of the European Communities which will identify (a) investment priorities in the region, selected on the basis of health impacts and cost-effectiveness criteria, for addressing local, transboundary (for example, acid rain), and global environmental problems; and (b) policy and institutional prerequisites for successful implementation of the action program. The study is being executed in collaboration with the Expert Group on Environment of the ECE and the Commission of the European Communities.

In parallel, a number of seminars on key topics, aimed at decisionmakers, are being arranged. A conference in Warsaw in May 1992, organized by the Bank in cooperation with the Organization for Economic Cooperation and Development (OECD) and the European Bank for Reconstruction and Development (EBRD), gave environmental officials from Central and Eastern Europe a first opportunity to come together with privatization and finance officials to develop strategies for dealing with environmental problems in the course of switching to a more market-oriented economy.

Baltic Sea Environmental Program. The Bank is an active member of a task force that presented to the environmental ministers of the Baltic countries a comprehensive action program intended to serve as the basis for a twenty-year action program to restore the ecology of the Baltic Sea's catchment area. The program includes policy actions and support for specific investments to improve water quality in rivers and coastal areas, protect wetlands, sustain fisheries, and enhance recreation and tourism.

The program's key activities will include (a) adoption of strengthened environmental policies, enforceable standards, and economic incentives; (b) the building up of local capacity to plan, finance, and implement environmental management activities; (c) emergency support for the continued operation of existing water and wastewater treatment systems; (d) preparation of feasibility studies for high-priority investments; (e) actions to upgrade municipal and industrial waste treatment facilities; (f) policy and investment options to address air quality problems affecting the region; (g) policy and investment activities to reduce agricultural runoff and the environmental impacts of large-scale livestock-breeding operations; (h) development of management programs for the conservation of coastal lagoons and wetlands; and (i) support for applied research and for public awareness campaigns.

Black Sea Environmental Management Program. With the support of the GEF partners, the Bank has initiated an environmental management program for the Black Sea, in cooperation with the littoral states—Bulgaria, Georgia, Romania, the Russian Federation, Turkey, and Ukraine. The project's main purpose is to identify and address the principal sources of pollution of the Black and Azov seas, which has resulted in extreme eutrophication and a drastic decline in fish populations and biodiversity. The $9.3 million contribution to core activities is viewed as seed money to mobilize funding from other sources to strengthen a broader program of support for the work and functions of the Black Sea Convention Commission.

The initial stage of the program will involve data collection to obtain a more comprehensive picture of the sources and biological effects of pollution. Information will be gathered on nutrient loads, waste stream discharges, inflows of fresh water from feeder rivers (the Danube, Dnepr, Dnestr, Don, and Kuban), coastal marine pollution from industries and municipalities, the offshore dumping of wastes, and the extent of over-fishing. The action program, expected to be launched in 1993, will support institution-building capacities within the littoral states, concentrating on environmental monitoring and analysis. It will also identify cost-effective investments to be undertaken by the countries around the Black Sea.

Economic and Sector Work

Resources for environmental investments are extremely scarce, and donor support is limited in relation to the requirements. The crucial premise underlying the region's economic and sector work is not simply to identify environmental investments but to encourage client countries to capture the benefits of broad economic policies. Specifically, this strategy implies further strong efforts to promote market reforms, emphasizing appropriate energy and natural resource pricing. Strengthening environmental institutions, regulatory policies, and related activities is another important element. Careful consideration is also given to the need to phase in environmental compliance strategies in parallel with economic restructuring.

The Bank has been engaged in an active dialogue with countries in the region and with donor countries on setting priorities and developing innovative approaches, usually beginning with preparation of individual country environmental strategy papers and related action plans. Special efforts have also been made to increase collaboration with local NGOs and universities in the development of environmental strategies. A first round of environmental strategy papers for the countries of Eastern Europe, beginning with Poland in 1989 and also including Bulgaria, the Czech and Slovak Republic, Hungary, Romania, and Yugoslavia, is now largely complete. In addition, an environmental action plan for Cyprus is nearing completion, and a strategy paper for Albania is being prepared.

These studies provide a broad overview of the main environmental issues (including economic factors such as resource pricing), identify "hot spots" of pollution where the impacts on human health appear most serious, and establish short- and medium-term priorities. They provide guidance for the Bank and other donors on priority investments. They also assess regulatory policies (a task that includes identifying opportunities for the introduction of economic incentives and market-based regulatory approaches) and institutional and training needs. Such sector work has in many cases been carried out jointly with the countries (including staff from governments, NGOs, and universities) and in some cases with donor countries. In addition, to provide information on cross-country experience, the regional Environment Division sponsored a report, completed this year, which reviews approaches to environmental management and institutional structures in selected OECD countries—France, Germany, the Netherlands, Sweden, the United Kingdom, and the United States.

Environmental sector work is continuing in the republics of the former U.S.S.R. Here, the Bank's approach has been to undertake the initial environmental analysis in the context of the first country economic memorandum, enabling the early establishment of links between environmental problems and the requirements of economic and industrial restructuring. These exercises have been particularly useful in highlighting the relationship of environmental problems to macroeconomic policies, resource pricing, and industrial restructuring. On the basis of these initial examinations, full environmental strategy studies have been launched in Belarus and Ukraine, and work is scheduled to begin soon in the Russian Federation.

The Bank also plans to address the environmental problems in the Aral Sea region through a concerted program that involves the five affected republics and is based in part on the experience of the Environmental Program for International Waters (covering the Mediterranean Sea, the Baltic Sea, the Danube River, and the Black Sea). The ecological disaster of the Aral Sea, which has been caused by excessive withdrawal of water for irrigation purposes, offers an example of a rural-based structural problem that will need to be addressed through a long-term program of diversification away from irrigated agriculture as the main economic activity. This will entail institutional changes made in the course of market reforms, such as the transfer of land to private ownership, accompanied by the introduction of appropriate incentives to encourage more efficient use of the available water resources.

Lending Operations

The sector work discussed above has been an impetus for the design of environmental projects. Sector work led to the preparation and approval of a technical assistance project in Poland that provides support for environmental management activities, including institutional and policy development, and for monitoring and evaluation. Currently, another generation of environmental projects is being developed to link industrial restructuring and environmental protection. One example is the innovative Coal Restructuring and Environment Project in Poland, now in preparation.

The region has few projects that are solely environmental, mainly because of borrowing countries' reluctance to invest in technical assistance and non-income-generating activities, but also because of institutional constraints. Environmental issues, being cross-sectoral, are difficult to address outside the context of targeted sectoral operations. But two projects approved during the year do have environmental components.

The Power and Environmental Improvement Project in the Czech and Slovak Republic is the product of recent energy and environmental sector work. This $246 million loan includes $140 million for flue gas desulfurization equipment at a large power plant burning high-sulfur brown coal in a heavily polluted region of Bohemia and $70 million for reduction of particulate emissions at the power plant and other plants in the area.

The Southeast Coast Sewerage and Drainage Project covers three towns along the picturesque southeast coast of Cyprus. Among the project's primary objectives are to provide safe and urgently needed sewerage systems for disposing of municipal and commercial wastewater that was fouling coastal areas and reducing tourist revenue; to provide a stormwater drainage system aimed at reducing intermittent flooding; to contribute to improved environmental management by promoting optimal reuse of treated wastewater and sludge; and to strengthen the institutional capacity of local "sewerage boards" in the three project towns.

Members of the Commonwealth of Independent States have only recently joined the Bank, and consequently lending for major projects has not yet begun. An environmental impact assessment seminar, funded by a Bank technical cooperation agreement, was held in June 1992. Its objective was to offer supplementary training in environmental impact assessment to selected specialists from the former U.S.S.R. The Bank has also made an effort to increase collaboration with local NGOs in planning and implementing projects in the area.

Through the end of the decade, the Bank will continue its efforts to provide substantial financial support for addressing environmental problems in those areas where market reforms and restructuring alone are likely to have little impact. This implies an emphasis on projects that focus on air quality management (for example, development of natural gas resources, restructuring in the power and coal sectors, provision of natural gas infrastructure for the household sector, and selected industrial investments, especially in metallurgy) and on special locations where water quality and hazardous wastes pose an immediate threat to human health and productivity. It will also involve contributing to the maintenance of existing infrastructure that affects water quality. As river basin management and municipal institutions become effective, the emphasis will increasingly shift toward new investments in wastewater and solid waste management.

The Bank is paying particular attention to the need for institutional strengthening (including donor coordination) and development of human resources. Such measures are critical for the longer-term implementation of sustainable environmental programs. This was recognized during the early stages of environmental work in Central Europe, when the Bank approved support for an environmental management project in Poland. Efforts will continue—especially under the GEF—to provide support for a few selected small-scale, but cost-effective, nature conservation activities to help prevent the deterioration of relatively untouched areas.

Projects under the Global Environment Facility

In December 1991 the grant agreement for the $4.5 million Poland Forest Biodiversity Protection Project was signed, making it the first GEF project approved by the Bank. Bank projects under preparation for the Europe and Central Asia region for which GEF cofinancing will be sought total $52.3 million. Projects that address global warming account for 69 percent of the grants and projects for the protection of biodiversity for 31 percent. Among these projects are grants totaling $6 million to Romania and Ukraine for the conservation and management of the Danube Delta and a $25 million grant to Poland for conversion of a district heating system from coal to gas.

The Bank is also the executing agency for two GEF projects sponsored by the UNDP: an $8.5 million project to manage the Danube River basin (an additional $15 million is coming from Austria, Germany, and Russia, see box 4-5) and the $10 million Black Sea Environmental Management Program.

Middle East and North Africa

Although the Middle East and North Africa is a large region, the distribution of water resources and arable land has drawn the region's popu-

Box 4-5. Sustainable Management of the Danube River Basin

With a total length of more than 2,000 kilometers, the Danube is the largest river in Western and Central Europe, and its basin is home to about 80 million people. The river is an important source of fresh water and is used for drinking, irrigation, fishing, energy and industrial production, transport, and waste disposal.

At the mouth of the Danube where it flows into the Black Sea is the Danube Delta. With its large areas of reed beds, maze of tributaries and canals, lakes rich with aquatic plants, and mosaic of forests, grasslands, and dunes, the delta forms a unique and complex ecosystem. It covers about 1 million hectares, spanning parts of Romania and, to a lesser extent, Ukraine, and provides vital habitats for a wide variety of wildlife, including about 350 species of birds, some of which are rare or endangered. It contains most of the world population of two endangered species, the pygmy cormorant and the red-breasted goose.

Overuse and misuse of the Danube's waters has led to widespread pollution, degraded riverine ecosystems, and depletion of fish stocks. Industrial and municipal effluents have lowered the quality of drinking water, especially in highly polluted tributaries such as the Tisza River. The Danube has a fundamental impact on the Black Sea, contributing half of the water running into the sea each year. The pollution load from the Danube has increased drastically in the past decade, triggering algal blooms and eutrophication. Pollution in the Black Sea has seriously affected fisheries and tourism, especially in the northern and western sections.

Recent developments have created a unique opportunity to save the Danube from further deterioration. In February 1992 the GEF partners—the UNDP, the UNEP, and the World Bank—in collaboration with the riparian states and other funding agencies, initiated the Environmental Program for the Danube River Basin. GEF support is provided through an $8.5 million grant, complemented by $500,000 from the Bank's Special Grants Program. Since the quality of the Danube's water has a definite impact on the biodiversity of the delta and the Black Sea coast, the Danube River Basin Study is being coordinated with two other GEF-sponsored programs, the Black Sea Environmental Management Program and the Danube Delta Biodiversity Project.

The river basin program includes (a) identification of areas and sources of pollution (both specific and dispersed); (b) development of a long-term strategic action plan for environmental protection and natural resource management (including cost estimates for implementation); (c) identification and preparation of preinvestment studies; and (d) improvement of national capacities for environmental monitoring and data management,

(Box continues on the following page.)

60

Box 4-5 (continued)

harmonization of environmental standards, and promotion of the exchange of data and technical information; (e) actions to protect biological reserves; and (f) support for strengthening local NGOs.

The Danube Delta plays a vital role in filtering out pollutants from the Danube as the river enters the Black Sea. Increasing pollution loads from the Danube, however, have overburdened this filtering capacity and are threatening the ecological balance on which this function is based. Roughly one-third of the delta's wetlands have been converted into managed forests, croplands and orchards, fishponds, and villages. As a result, the region's biodiversity has deteriorated, and the delta's effectiveness as a filter has been seriously impaired.

A separate GEF grant of $6 million will contribute to the formulation of a long-term management plan for the delta. The grant would support the following activities: establishing the basis for ecological and hydrologic modeling and developing an information system for management and applied research; launching staff training programs, particularly for improving the effectiveness of policing; implementing and monitoring a number of pilot rehabilitation measures; developing an investment strategy for restoration of wetland ecosystems; and initiating local community support programs, including environmental education and awareness programs.

---

lation of 230 million toward coastal areas and river valleys. This phenomenon, along with a corresponding concentration of industry, agriculture, and transport activities, has created unique population growth rates and complex patterns of rural-urban migration. Key environmental challenges are the scarcity and degradation of water resources, the pollution of the urban environment (most of it coastal), the degradation of land and forest resources, and the neglect of regional commons.

Water quality issues in the region are associated with increasing treatment and health costs and, when large bodies of water are subjected to mistreatment over prolonged periods, to a loss of economic use through damage to fisheries, tourism, and wildlife resources. Municipal and industrial wastes dumped into wetlands, urban landfills, and storage sites for toxic materials leach into the groundwater, where toxins accumulate. Among the many examples of emerging water quality problems are:

- Nile River measurements at various monitoring stations that show fecal and coliform bacteria at 2,000 times European standards

- Nitrate levels in Algeria's Mitidja aquifer that, at 40 percent of all monitoring stations, exceed the limits recommended by the World Health Organization
- At the King Talal Dam in Jordan, high levels of bacterial and chemical pollutants that make the water unfit to drink.

Problems of water contamination by industry, particularly dispersed small and medium-scale industry, are especially complex because of the difficulties of monitoring pollution, enforcing standards, and predicting the viability of outmoded industry if environmental controls were required. Large-scale industry, which may be easier to monitor, is not easier to control. Problems with phosphates in Tunisia, sugar mills that dump wastes into the Sebou River in Morocco, mercury pollution in Algeria and Egypt, and cement dust in Egypt are all associated with parastatal ownership of industries.

Pressures on land and forest resources are also directly related to the scarcity and quality of water resources. It is estimated that 10 percent of Tunisia's agricultural land has been affected by erosion; in Morocco the figure is as high as 40 percent. Pastures, which cover 20 percent of the region's lands, are under pressure from increasing numbers of livestock, reducing productivity and leading to degradation of soils and increased desertification. Creative approaches are being sought to reduce overgrazing, increase carrying capacity and animal productivity, and, where necessary, reduce stocks. It appears that forest resources, limited as they are in the region, are gradually being replaced at a rate that now roughly equals the rate of deforestation. Afforestation programs to counter forest loss are particularly notable in the Maghreb, but the problem of species loss still persists.

The concentration of industry around major urban centers gives rise to a large part of urban air pollution in the region. Cairo and Alexandria account for 95 percent of the major polluters in Egypt and for 77 percent of all heavy industry. In Iran a similar concentration is found around Tehran; industries are found around Casablanca and Mohamedia in Morocco, around Algiers and Oran in Algeria, and around Gabes and Sfax in Tunisia. The energy intensity of industry in the region is high, but those countries that price energy close to world levels have energy intensities five to ten times lower than those that do not.

Strategic Priorities

WATER. Water scarcity and the mounting pollution of available surface water will continue to be the main environmental concern in many of the region's countries. The key environmental issues are the reduced quantities available for human consumption and the severe water quality problems that are emerging from a combination of low supply, inadequate municipal treatment, high agricultural runoff, and uncontrolled effluents from industry.

Increasing water demand—a result of rapidly growing populations and industrial expansion—implies difficult choices: reducing the quantity of water available to agriculture, mining fossil aquifers, or undertaking costly desalination technologies and recycling. Fortunately, available evidence suggests the large scope for increasing the efficiency of water use, particularly in irrigation, through proper pricing signals and incentives. Such incentives for increased efficiency do not exist uniformly and are further limited by cultural and institutional constraints. Nevertheless, strategic policies to promote more efficient water use, more reliable water supplies, and improved water quality will be critical for the overall economic development of the region.

Egypt, which derives more than 95 percent of its total water needs from the Nile River, is perhaps the most compelling example in the region of a country in which water problems have adversely affected other sectors of the economy, notably agriculture. At a time when water consumption per capita is rising, the Nile is fouled with untreated industrial and municipal wastes, and many parts are saline because of the leaching of salts from irrigated fields. Nearly one-third of Egypt's irrigated fields are now salinized and in need of costly reclamation.

URBANIZATION. Urbanization also poses serious environmental challenges for the future. Large cities are the norm, with 27 percent of the population already living in the capital cities. Tehran is projected to become the world's seventh largest city by 2010, and by 2000 Cairo will have a population density of 40,000 per square kilometer. (Bangkok today has 21,000 per square kilometer.) The rapid growth of these megacities creates an enormous need for management of water, wastewater, and solid waste. Industrial pollution and vehicle emissions lead to serious air quality problems. Urban waste disposal services are inadequate in all the major urban centers of the region. Removal of biological pollutants is one of the most important urban environmental priorities, followed by initiatives to improve air quality.

COASTAL RESOURCES. The other major environmental challenge is the sustainable management of coastal resources, particularly along the Mediterranean, the Red Sea, and the Gulf. Most coastal cities in this region are growing faster than urban areas in the interior. Exploding populations are contributing to a breakdown in crucial services, including the provision of adequate housing, clean water, and sanitation.

Coastal waters throughout the region are increasingly polluted with untreated municipal and industrial effluents. In the eastern Mediterranean and the northern parts of the Red Sea, chronic oil pollution from offshore drilling and routine shipping are of growing concern. Inadequate tourism infrastructure and pollution control measures threaten to undermine tourism, which is an important source of foreign exchange for many North African and Middle East countries, especially those on the southern rim of the Mediterranean.

NEW INITIATIVES. Regional activities form a crucial component of the Bank's new initiatives in North Africa and the Middle East. They offer opportunities for the Bank to share and synthesize its experience in individual countries and to suggest common solutions to common problems. The regional program draws heavily on the substantial policy and investment work undertaken by the Bank in collaboration with member countries and other organizations.

An important ongoing activity is the Mediterranean Environmental Technical Assistance Program (METAP; see box 4-6) which supports regional environmental programs and training, as well as the preparation of investment projects to be considered for Bank financing. In addition to a second phase of METAP, regional activities under preparation include the Gulf Environmental Action Plan and a regional plan for the Red Sea.

Economic and Sector Work

Leading the environmental sector work this year is a recently completed environmental action plan for Egypt. Prepared in cooperation with local working groups, it identifies economic policy changes (for example, improved resource pricing and structural changes to encourage greater accountability by enterprises) and needs for institutional strengthening, all of which are crucial for an effective environmental strategy. It also identifies priority technical assistance and investments over the short to long term, generating project ideas for the Bank and numerous other donors.

Fundamental to the Bank's environmental strategy for the region is the concept that the environment agenda is to be a fully integrated theme in current and future Bank lending activities, rather than a procedural hurdle. In line with the "win-win" approach advocated by *World Development Report 1992*, the regional strategy aims at demonstrating the overlap between the development and environmental agendas through joint analytical and strategic work and public participation. Thus, the region is launching a process to include the findings of environmental work in the next round of country economic memoranda and country

Box 4-6. Helping to Save the Mediterranean

The Mediterranean Environmental Technical Assistance Program is a major component of the Environmental Program for the Mediterranean, an initiative launched in 1990 by the European Investment Bank (EIB) and the World Bank to curb and try to reverse trends of environmental degradation in the Mediterranean. The first pilot cycle of METAP (1990–92), funded by the Commission of the European Communities, the EIB, the UNDP, and the World Bank, is now drawing to a close. Its budget has been fully committed, and many activities have been completed or are nearing completion.

The success of this first cycle has led to increased demand for participation in the program on the national, regional, and subregional levels. In response to this demand, donors have agreed to pursue a second three-year cycle with enlarged geographic coverage of Mediterranean countries. The second cycle is likely to increase emphasis on the coastal urban environment and step up regional efforts on common environmental issues.

During the past year METAP's balanced approach of launching and implementing project preparation activities, policy studies, and institutional development activities concurrently has been introduced throughout the region. Activities begun in fiscal 1992 include, in Algeria, Blida Wastewater Reuse and a management plan for El Kala National Park; in Tunisia, Pilot Wastewater Reuse, which is looking at the feasibility of marketing wastewater, sludge, and compost; and in Turkey, Marmara Maritime Pollution Control, which is devising an effective management system to enforce pollution prevention measures in the Sea of Marmara, the Dardanelles, and the Bosphorus. Activities developed under METAP are increasingly being introduced into lending activities of the World Bank and the European Investment Bank; two have led to GEF financing.

In the area of policy studies, the Environmental Financing study has been completed, and a regional workshop in which all Mediterranean countries participated was held in December 1991. The workshop reviewed the OECD's experience with environmental financing, as well as specific national studies completed in Tunisia, Turkey, and Yugoslavia. The Environmental Fiscal Instruments policy study for Cyprus was launched to develop appropriate fiscal mechanisms for implementing sound land use policies and coastal zone management practices.

Three regional networks, initiated in the context of METAP's institutional development component, were all active during the past year: MEDCITIES, which links Mediterranean coastal cities; MEDNEA, the Mediterranean National Environmental Agencies Network; and MEDPAN, the Mediterranean Protected Areas Network. MED POL, the UNEP's Mediterranean Pollution Monitoring and Research Programme, is also supported by METAP. Training seminars on coastal environmental impact assessment have been held in several countries.

strategy papers, starting with those for Egypt, Tunisia, and Yemen. In addition, selected pieces of analytical work in traditional sectors (especially industry, energy, and infrastructure) have been identified for special attention in raising environmental issues and suggesting solutions as part of overall sector strategy.

The following are key elements of the regional strategy:

- Ensuring that the *environmental impact* of Bank-financed projects in the current lending program is well understood and that mitigation is undertaken. There is a regional commitment to strengthening this function by supplementing skills, offering in-house training, and further reinforcing the review processes. EIA training for borrowers has been organized by the Bank in Morocco and Tunisia, and special EIA units are being created in these countries. Similar efforts are now being made in Algeria and Egypt. Following a recent portfolio reclassification in the region, environmental assessments have increased significantly.

- Obtaining a clear understanding of the *nature of the environmental challenge* in each country, including opportunities for intersectoral collaboration. Local capacity building is an essential part of this process. It is being achieved through the preparation of national environmental action plans, building on the successful models of Tunisia (1990) and Egypt (1992).

- Closely examining the *urban-environment-poverty nexus*—the interplay of rapid urbanization, concentration of poorly regulated industry, and inefficient transport, focusing on its income-regressive features. These interrelationships pose a serious challenge in Tehran and Cairo. The regional strategy envisages launching in fiscal 1993 an initial effort on urban problems that could eventually include environmental audits in the major cities of the region, depending on cofinancing, and would influence the design of future lending programs.

- Rethinking *water management issues.* Although quantity is the main water issue in the region, it is necessary to reinforce the links of that issue with water quality and health. The regional goal is to define a water resources management strategy, including review of how countries might better manage their wastes, and to propose a strategy for future Bank activities in the region. This strategy, to be completed by the end of 1992, will call for comprehensive country-based water resources assessments to review the main aspects of water planning and management, including institutional arrangements, supply and demand management, and investment strategy.

- Generating an interest in the medium-term importance of *regional and global environmental issues*. Clearer understanding is needed of the global-warming phenomenon as it relates to the region. The strategy would also enlarge the scope of North-South and regional collaboration, such as that established for the Mediterranean under METAP. The region is committed to supporting similar initiatives for the Red Sea and the Gulf, particularly under an expanded GEF program. The regional strategy also calls for continued close collaboration with other donors and agencies, especially the Commission of the European Communities, the European Investment Bank, the UNDP, and the UNEP, to leverage the Bank's limited resources and minimize the management burdens on emerging environmental institutions in borrower countries.

Environmental issues have figured prominently in other sector work as well, notably in agriculture and forestry (for example, in Yemen). Finally, a working document on the environment, prepared for Morocco in 1991, led to further dialogue with the government and to the development of an environmental management project for fiscal 1993.

Lending Operations

Environmental and related sector work led to the creation of four projects with environmental components:

- A $32.8 million credit for the Land and Water Conservation Project in Yemen has environmental components to improve water distribution for controlled irrigation, expand sand dune stabilization and soil protection efforts, conserve key native forest areas, preserve biodiversity, and promote afforestation schemes. Other aims are to strengthen participating institutions and agencies and establish strong fiscal incentives, such as the elimination of environmentally harmful subsidies and the levy of appropriate water charges.
- A $75 million loan in support of Tunisia's Municipal Sector Investment Project will improve infrastructure and municipal services in a number of cities and towns with an aggregate population of about 5 million. It includes a $20.7 million environmental component for improved management of liquid and solid wastes, sanitation services, sound disposal of slaughterhouse offal and other food-processing wastes, and street maintenance activities to facilitate road transport and reduce dust levels in city centers.
- In Iran a $57 million loan in support of the Sistan River Flood Works Rehabilitation Project has environmental components aimed at

strengthening the implementing agency's institutional capacity to maintain flood protection works more effectively through, among other activities, the development and implementation of a resource management plan.

- The Sahara Regional Development Project for Algeria (supported by a $57 million loan) addresses the institutional need for an infrastructural and monitoring system for water resource use, water and soil quality, and drainage. The environmental components of the institution-strengthening project provide technical assistance and training in the preparation of environmental assessments for future investments.

Projects under the Global Environment Facility and the Montreal Protocol

GEF projects in preparation for the region in fiscal 1992 include $10 million to the Maghreb countries of North Africa for protection of marine habitats against oil spills, $4.75 million to Egypt for protection of Red Sea coral reefs from pollution, and $2 million to Iran for a study to reduce energy demand in urban transport—a demonstration project related to global warming.

Individual country strategies for phasing out CFCs, in support of the Montreal Protocol, are also being prepared. Grants have been awarded to Egypt, Jordan, and Tunisia, mostly for converting to non-CFC refrigerants. A critical question for the Bank is how to incorporate investments for phasing out CFCs—which may tend to be small manufacturing subprojects—into Bank lending programs.

Latin America and the Caribbean

The Latin America and Caribbean region includes thirty countries with a total population of nearly 450 million. The population of the region is growing by less than 2 percent a year and will double in about thirty-seven years if current growth rates continue. As the demographic transition takes hold, birthrates across the region continue to drop as more and more women get access to family planning and maternal and child health care services. In South America, the total fertility rate—the average number of children a woman has over her reproductive life—has dropped from 4.6 in the early 1970s to 3.2 today.

Latin American cities are expanding rapidly as populations concentrate in the region's urban areas. By 2000, the United Nations has estimated, 77 percent of Latin America's population will be urbanized. Three of the ten largest cities in the world—Buenos Aires, Mexico City, and São Paulo—are in this region, and two of them, Mexico City and São Paulo, are among the most polluted cities on earth.

Economic growth in the region is beginning to recover as several countries have stabilized their economies and are adopting needed structural reforms. Future growth prospects, however, are jeopardized by a complex set of environmental and natural resource management problems. Forest and habitat destruction, which can lead to the displacement or disruption of Amerindian communities, has accompanied the expansion of the "economic frontier," resulting in biodiversity loss, falling agricultural productivity, and the loss of forests' carbon-absorbing capacities.

Twenty-eight of the thirty countries in the region have coastal resources—coral reefs, mangrove forests, and seagrass beds—on which they depend for tourism, aquaculture and mariculture, fishing, and other economic activities. But coastal ecosystems are under tremendous pressure from development, and their productivity is threatened by pollution from industries and municipalities, agricultural runoff, sedimentation from logging operations and coastal development, offshore oil production, improper land use, and overfishing.

Most countries in the region have started to address their environmental problems. Initiatives include reforms of policies that contribute to environmental degradation (such as subsidized power and irrigation projects), strengthened legislation, better monitoring and enforcement, and assessment and mitigation of the environmental impacts of public sector projects. The challenges that remain, however, are enormous by any standard. Although capacities to meet these challenges vary widely, most countries are still ill-prepared.

Strategic Priorities

The Bank's strategy in the region emphasizes three major themes: strengthening environmental institutions; setting clear priorities; and encouraging efficient approaches to resource management.

INSTITUTION STRENGTHENING. Lack of institutional capacity is the most serious impediment to improved environmental management. Most countries have inadequate or unenforced laws for environmental protection, weak or nonexistent environmental institutions, poorly trained staff, incomplete data collection and analysis, and poor monitoring and enforcement of existing laws and regulations. Although important environmental policy changes can be implemented within existing institutional structures (see box 4-7), improved environmental management will need careful nurturing, underscored by the development of appro-

Box 4-7. Anticipating the Environmental Costs of Energy Projects in Colombia

Electric power generation in Colombia is predominantly hydroelectric (about 70 percent) and coal-fired thermal. To date, less than 10 percent of Colombia's potential hydroelectric capacity has been tapped, even though the country has a well-developed national electricity grid. As a result, there are many different options for future hydroelectric schemes, some of which would be much less environmentally damaging per unit of electricity produced than others. For example, the recently completed 1,600-megawatt Guavio project floods only 1,500 hectares of mostly deforested land, with virtually no off-site environmental impacts. By contrast, the proposed 860-megawatt Urra II project would inundate nearly 70,000 hectares, most of which is primary tropical forest. Careful project siting is also important for minimizing environmental damage from thermal power stations burning fossil fuels.

The Colombian government is taking important and innovative steps to incorporate environmental considerations into its Least-Cost Investment Program. Under this project, Interconexion Electrica S.A. (ISA), the country's leading energy agency, has developed an ingenious methodology for partially internalizing the environmental costs of expanding the country's power generation and distribution network. In phase I, each proposed hydroelectric scheme is ranked and rated according to thirty-one quantitative environmental indicators, which are normalized so that all hydropower projects can be compared on the same scale. Since these indicators tend to be self-reinforcing, the same projects get consistently high (negative) environmental ratings regardless of which combination of indicators is used. Projects with very large, relatively shallow reservoirs, for example, tend to get environmentally negative scores on a wide range of indicators, including the amount of forest and cropland flooded, the number of people resettled, the susceptibility of the reservoir to rapid sedimentation, water quality problems, and effects on native fish populations.

The ISA has also developed a similar phase I methodology, involving about nineteen indicators, for environmental rating and ranking of new thermal power plants. (These rankings, however, do not compare the environmental tradeoffs of hydroelectric and thermal plants.) According to ISA staff, the environmental ratings derived from the phase I methodology were weighted "subjectively" against standard economic considerations in the selection of these projects. The more ambitious phase II methodology seeks to quantify the anticipated environmental costs of various proposed new power projects in economic terms so that these costs can be more precisely incorporated into the process of selecting new projects for the Least-Cost Investment Program.

(Box continues on the following page.)

Box 4-7 (continued)

The three hydroelectric projects chosen for the 1991–2000 investment program have relatively low or moderate environmental impacts. If the process initiated by the ISA for incorporating environmental considerations into power generation planning continues to be refined and implemented, it is likely that the most potentially damaging hydroelectric projects in Colombia will continue to be deferred indefinitely in favor of more environmentally benign ones.

---

priate institutions. The Bank supports the development of these institutions through lending and training. A number of countries have made promising starts, some with Bank assistance, but much remains to be done.

SETTING PRIORITIES. Given the environmental problems facing most of the countries in the region and the overall scarcity of resources available for addressing the problems, clear priorities need to be set. The highest priority should go to improving economic and environmental management. Subsidies for water, power, fertilizers and pesticides also subsidize environmental degradation, encourage economic waste, and strain national treasuries. Eliminating subsidies improves efficiency and macro-economic stability and reduces harmful environmental impacts. Clarifying and enforcing property rights can also pay high dividends in halting the degradation of "open-access" natural resources, such as forests, watersheds, and coastal wetlands.

RESOURCE MANAGEMENT. Although much can be done by eliminating distortions in macroeconomic and sectoral policies and clarifying property rights, these actions by themselves will not be enough. If environmental protection is to be adequate, resources must be devoted specifically to this end. This involves difficult tradeoffs, which are often best considered through a comparison of costs and benefits. In view of the region's trend towards heavy urbanization and the pervasiveness of urban pollution, the highest payoffs in much of Latin America and the Caribbean are likely to come from measures to improve urban water and sanitation services and reduce ambient atmospheric concentrations of pollutants associated with respiratory disease. Relatively high payoffs are also likely to be associated with solving environmental problems that directly impinge on productivity (for example, soil erosion in agricultural areas and upland watersheds and pollution of coastal waters).

The tight resource situation also requires efficient approaches to solving environmental problems. As a matter of strategy, this means employing policy leverage by, for example, eliminating subsidies that encourage pollution, clarifying property rights, and taxing the use of polluting inputs. Such an approach minimizes the costs of administering environmental protection programs and leaves decisions about resource allocation in the hands of the private decisionmakers who are best equipped to make them. At the program and project level, proposals need to be subjected to careful cost-benefit or cost-effectiveness analysis.

NEW INITIATIVES. The Earth Summit focused worldwide attention on Latin America and its environmental problems. The countries of the region responded to UNCED by renewing their commitment to improve environmental monitoring and management. The Bank is actively supporting this through a number of new initiatives, including strengthening its environmental staff and developing new lending programs to address both pollution and natural resource management issues.

This commitment is reflected in the addition of new staff to the regional Environment Division, the appointment of a senior adviser for agriculture and natural resources in the region's Technical Department, and the designation of environmental units in several country departments. In recognition of the importance of environmental issues in Brazil, the country department responsible for Brazil, Peru, and Venezuela has reformulated its agricultural division as the Environment and Agricultural Operations Division. The country operations division responsible for Mexico and Central America has also added a core environmental unit for similar reasons.

Institutional strengthening is important for borrower countries as well as for the Bank. In the future, more lending will go to institutional development projects, and components to strengthen environmental units are increasingly being incorporated in other lending operations. In this way both national-level, priority-setting institutions and specialized sectoral units (for example, in ministries of forestry, mining, or health) are being strengthened. Existing loans are helping Brazil, Chile, and Mexico develop their institutional capacity to manage the environment. Proposed future lending in this area includes projects in Ecuador, Nicaragua, and Venezuela, among others.

Project lending to address both pollution and natural resource management problems is increasing. In the work plan for the next few years are projects that will provide funds for management of national parks in Venezuela, water supply and sanitation activities in Chile, Costa Rica, Haiti, Peru, and Uruguay, and improved health and urban services in Argentina and in El Salvador.

Regional training in environmental assessment and environmental economics will also receive more attention in the future. A number of current and planned Bank-funded projects, among them recent loans to Chile and Mexico, include funding to support economic analysis of major environmental problems and policy issues. A regional conference on environmental issues that is being planned by the Bank will focus on the practical issues of institutionalizing environmental strategies. The legal and regulatory framework for environmental management is an important dimension of this process.

Economic and Sector Work

Several studies or components of studies were undertaken during the fiscal year to strengthen the Bank's advice to countries in the region concerning priorities and strategies and to lay the foundations for future lending operations. One study examines the costs associated with urban pollution in Santiago and in a number of Brazilian cities. The results will highlight the effects of urban pollution on human health, especially on the very young and the very old. Both air and water pollution impose significant social and economic costs. The ability of wealthier individuals to protect themselves from the effects of water pollution (less so from air pollution) has led to a relative underinvestment in potable water supply. Fairly modest investments in the control of water pollution may yield much larger returns than similar investments in control of air pollution. For example, effluent charges on polluting industries in São Paulo have helped reduce water demand by 40 to 60 percent, releasing more and cleaner water for household use.

Another study assessed the costs of a number of environmental problems in Mexico. Values were calculated for soil erosion, health costs from poor water quality and inadequate sanitation, and air pollution in the Mexico City Metropolitan Area. In some cases, the results supported common perceptions about the relative importance of different problems. Soil erosion, for example, was found to be a serious nationwide problem, causing production losses estimated at $1.2 billion a year. Other results were surprising. Previously, it had been assumed that ozone constituted the most serious threat to human health in Mexico City and other urban areas with heavy traffic. But new data revealed that the health costs associated with suspended particulates were potentially as much as $800 million a year—more than eight times greater than those attributed to ozone. And while the effects of polluted water and inadequate sanitation have long been accepted as critical problems, the study found that their health cost was in fact three times greater (about $3 billion) than the costs associated with urban air pollution in the Mexico City Metropolitan Area.

Internal Bank studies initiated or in progress during fiscal 1992 include a regional strategy for the next phase of GEF operations, an examination of the current and prospective roles played by frontier governments in the Amazon in protecting the environment, and an evaluation of the condition and needs of environmental institutions in the region.

Environmental issues are also being addressed in other parts of the economic and sector work program. Several country economic memoranda issued during the year—for example, for Antigua and Barbuda and for St. Vincent and the Grenadines—had chapters or sections devoted to the environment. These described recent country environmental trends, discussed priorities, and recommended practical approaches for confronting problems of environmental protection and resource management. Increasingly, the Bank's country strategies are also dealing specifically with environmental and natural resource management issues.

In preparation for UNCED, the region undertook a comprehensive assessment of its environmental work. The results of this assessment are contained in "Environment and Development in Latin America and the Caribbean: The Role of the World Bank" (World Bank 1992a).

Lending Operations

ENVIRONMENTAL PROJECTS. The $50 million loan for Mexico's Environmental Project supports the strengthening of Mexico's National Environmental Agency, SEDUE, and the development of decentralized policymaking. It finances key environmental services: monitoring and control of air and water pollution; strengthened environmental assessment capabilities; conservation of biodiversity; better management and administration; a pilot effort to decentralize environmental regulation; special studies to explore the use of economic instruments as a means of encouraging environmental protection; and the preparation of additional technical standards for pollution control and protection of natural resources.

In Brazil the National Industrial Pollution Control Project provides a $50 million line of credit through the National Economic and Social Development Bank (BNDES) for financing investments in the control of industrial pollution. The project also provides technical assistance to the state environmental agency and the BNDES. The Mato Grosso Natural Resources Management Project allocates $205 million for sustainable management of key resources such as watershed forests, fresh water, and minerals. To further its goal of strengthening forest management and conservation, the project supports environmental and tribal protection and small-farmer community projects. A $167 million Bank loan in support of the Rondônia Natural Resource Management Project includes more than $57 million for environmental protection efforts in Amazonia—land mapping, zoning, and regularization and the establishment and management of conservation units and Amerindian reserves.

In Haiti a $26.1 million credit for the Forestry and Environmental Protection Project provides technical and financial support for strengthening the country's institutions responsible for the management of forest resources. The project's specific forestry and environmental programs include the management of protected areas and the promotion of more efficient charcoal stoves to conserve scarce fuelwood.

PROJECTS WITH ENVIRONMENTAL COMPONENTS. The Argentina Hydrocarbon Sector Engineering Project will define environmental policies pertaining to the sector and will develop the government's capacity to regulate oil and gas exploration and production. The loan will also support government efforts to develop and implement environmental and safety standards.

In Brazil the Water Sector Modernization Project includes $8 million for institutionalizing environmental assessment of water and sewerage projects and promotes a better balance between investments in water supply and sewerage. The São Paulo Metropolitan Transport Decentralization Project, among its other objectives, would reduce emissions of air pollutants from the transport sector by encouraging a shift to mass transit, promoting cleaner fuels, and improving the flow of traffic.

The Chile Transport Infrastructure Project allocates $1.1 million to environmental improvements at several seaports. It will include an action plan that addresses potential problems from ships' wastes, spills, or hazardous cargoes. The port administration intends to grant concessions to private enterprises to equip ports with proper waste disposal facilities, including oil-water separators for reclaiming oily wastes and bilge slops from ships. These enterprises will charge for the services they provide.

In Colombia the Third National Roads Sector Project will support the establishment of an environmental unit in the Ministry of Public Works and Transportation, as well as technical assistance studies and training in environmental assessment, in an effort to reduce the impacts of road construction and maintenance activities.

In Costa Rica the Agricultural Sector Investment and Institutional Development Project will support the improvement of land use classification, identify ecosystems susceptible to soil loss and measure the extent and cost of actual or potential damage to the natural resource base, demarcate the boundaries of national parks, and support land titling and consolidation of smallholder agricultural settlements.

The Honduras Energy Sector Adjustment Credit Program, in addition to supporting measures to make the country's energy sector more efficient, includes technical assistance components for petroleum exploration and related environmental protection regulations and a study of fuel substitution that will address, among other matters, concerns about deforestation caused by excessive use of fuelwood.

In Mexico the Irrigation and Drainage Sector Project earmarks $49 million for environmental components. This loan will help institutionalize environmental assessment as a necessary step in the development of the government's investment program for the irrigation sector and will support a program of environmental studies.

In Paraguay the Land Use Rationalization Project will initiate the establishment of a Geographic Information System (GIS) for land use classification, as well as studies aimed at the rationalization of land use and the strengthening of institutions involved with natural resource management. The studies will include a detailed analysis of the legal framework and drafts of appropriate environmental legislation and regulations.

In Trinidad and Tobago the Business Expansion and Industrial Restructuring Project supports the development of an improved set of environmental pollution control standards and mitigation measures for screening public and private investment projects. The project will also strengthen the government's capacity to review environmental impact assessments.

During fiscal 1992 institution-building and -reinforcing projects were under development in Bolivia, Chile, Colombia, and Ecuador. These projects will support enactment or rationalization of environmental legislation, the setting of standards and regulations, monitoring and enforcement, and improvement of the management and administrative capacity of environmental agencies. In Bolivia, for example, the loan will help the central government build the institutional capacity to deal with environmental issues in all sectors. The credit will support technical assistance and training in environmental planning and management, training in environmental impact assessment, establishment of an environmental data system, and promulgation and enforcement of environmental quality regulations. It should enable Bolivia to deal with a range of difficult problems, such as the environmental impact of mining.

Environmental Action Plans

Environmental action plans, or their functional equivalents, have been completed or are under way in a number of the region's countries. These include Bolivia, Brazil, Chile, Dominica, Dominican Republic, Ecuador, El Salvador, Grenada, Guatemala, Guyana, Haiti, Honduras, Mexico, Nicaragua, Paraguay, Peru, St. Kitts and Nevis, St. Lucia, and St. Vincent and the Grenadines.

Projects under the Global Environment Facility, the Montreal Protocol, and the Rainforest Trust Fund

At the end of fiscal 1992 the region had twelve projects approved or in preparation under the auspices of the GEF, six under the Montreal Protocol, and two under the Rainforest Trust Fund.

Reflecting the rich diversity and importance of the region's fauna and flora, the GEF portfolio is weighted heavily in favor of biodiversity projects. The Mexico Conservation Units Project, for example, which was approved as a component of the Mexico National Environment Project, provides up to $30 million of GEF support for investments to protect Mexico's most important areas of biodiversity and for the preparation of management plans. The management plans for each area covered by the project divide the respective areas into strict conservation zones and buffer zones (patterned after the United Nations Educational, Scientific and Cultural Organization's—UNESCO's—Man and the Biosphere Program). The buffer zones are intended to allow for rational and sustainable economic utilization of protected resources, balancing development objectives with conservation priorities. Biodiversity conservation projects in Brazil, Bolivia, Ecuador, and Peru were at an advanced stage of preparation at the end of fiscal 1992; approvals are anticipated in early fiscal 1993.

Three GEF global-warming projects were under consideration during the year. Two—in Jamaica and Mexico—would strengthen institutions for demand-side management and demonstrate potentially useful demand-side management technologies. The third project, Brazil Biomass Gasification with Gas Turbines, would cofinance the construction and demonstration of a combined-cycle gas turbine generator fueled by gasified biomass.

Two GEF projects that deal with pollution in the Caribbean are also under preparation. The Organization of Eastern Caribbean States (OECS) Waste Management Project, which is associated with an IBRD/IDA-financed project for the OECS countries, is a demonstration project in support of annex V of the MARPOL Convention. It is intended to protect the islands' coastal zones and surrounding waters from further degradation by focusing on the management of solid and liquid wastes. The second project, the Wider Caribbean Initiative for Disposal of Ship-Generated Waste, would develop and cofinance a comprehensive region-wide approach toward making investments and constructing a regulatory framework for handling both solid and liquid wastes under annex V of the MARPOL Convention.

Under Montreal Protocol funding, country programs designed to phase out ozone-depleting substances were approved for Ecuador and Mexico; plans in Brazil, Chile and Venezuela are being prepared. Mexico's program considers the possible use of marketable permits as an instrument for efficiently rationing supplies of ozone-depleting chemicals during the country's accelerated phaseout period. Investment projects to support phaseout activities were approved for Mexico, and funds to undertake preinvestment feasibility studies were approved for Ecuador.

At a meeting in Geneva in early December 1991 a number of donor countries expressed their support for a Pilot Program to Conserve the Brazilian Rainforest and pledged to support such a program through contributions to a trust fund to be administered by the Bank and through associated bilateral cofinancing arrangements. Following the Geneva meeting, Bank staff finalized a document laying out the institutional framework and establishing conditions on the basis of the views of the donors and the government of Brazil. Program participants ratified this document, and on March 24, 1992, the Executive Directors of the World Bank approved a resolution establishing a Rainforest Trust Fund (RFT) to provide financing for projects under the pilot phase. To date, donors have pledged about $55 million to the RFT and have also pledged more than $200 million in associated bilateral aid. Within the Bank the pilot program is being administered by Latin America and Caribbean Country Department I, which has established a coordinating office in the Environment and Agriculture Operations Division for this purpose.

Of the several projects to be prepared and implemented under the pilot program, two are in an advanced stage of preparation. The first, the Indigenous Reserves Project, would finance the demarcation of indigenous reserves in the Brazilian Amazon and would support sustainable management of natural resources in those areas. The second, Demonstration Projects involving grass-roots groups, would test new technologies and development strategies aimed at improving the standard of living for residents of Brazil's Amazon region without damaging the rainforest. Other projects under the pilot program would support environmental policy projects, conservation units, scientific research, management of natural resources, and environmental education.

5. Policy and Research

This section describes the key elements of the Bank's environmental research and policy work in fiscal 1992. *World Development Report 1992* drew on these and other studies to present the Bank's current understanding of the links between environment and development and of the principles and practice of good policymaking for sustainable development. The report was widely disseminated in the lead-up to the Earth Summit and subsequently. To date, seminars and press conferences have been presented in about fifty countries. Active publications and dissemination programs also exist for the Bank's other research products.

This year, policy and research emphasized the incorporation of environmental issues into a broad spectrum of sectoral and cross-sectoral economic policy work: economic valuation and analysis; poverty reduction; energy use and efficiency; the pollution-related "brown agenda" of urban areas in developing countries; sound marine and coastal zone management; and sustainable agriculture and forestry. In comparison with previous years, research activities placed more emphasis on social and cultural issues, such as the role of women as natural resource managers, the treatment of indigenous peoples, and the challenges of equitable resettlement practices. Increasingly, research is aimed at improving environmental information, which is essential for sound environmental assessment and for sound decisionmaking regarding development.

Environmental Economics

Overriding this year's research agenda for environmental economics is the issue of how to value environmental "goods" and "bads," for which few markets exist. Positive outcomes of analytical research and applied case studies have enabled the Bank to prepare training workshops, seminars, and documents on environmental economics and its application in various sectors.

Economic Valuation of Environmental Impacts

CASE STUDIES AND RESEARCH. Two case studies of developing countries and a comprehensive dissemination program were key elements of economic valuation work. A case study for Madagascar sought a better understanding of the impact of national parks management on the country's tropical forests. Both conventional and innovative economic techniques were used to evaluate damage to forests and watersheds, timber and nontimber benefits, health effects and other impacts on local inhabitants, impacts on biodiversity, and ecotourism benefits. Policy recommendations are being developed on the basis of specific environmental-economic interactions examined in the study.

The other case study considers the incorporation of environmental impacts into energy sector decisionmaking and examines Sri Lanka's electric power expansion plan. The integrated energy-environmental analysis will help improve project design and eliminate projects with unacceptable impacts. In some instances, multiple criteria evaluation techniques were used to supplement conventional cost-benefit analysis. Areas of study included the tradeoffs among coal, oil, hydroelectric, and nonconventional energy sources, as well as reduction of system losses, end-use conservation, pricing policy, and demand management.

Economic valuation of land resource management continued in fiscal 1992. A senior-level methodological workshop reviewed various models of farmers' resource use and of the application of analytical tools in developing countries, particularly in Africa. Other work included the refinement of resource models in a field-level case study of the Machakos district in Kenya (see also "Land Degradation and Sustainable Agriculture," below).

Recently completed research on the production and trade impacts of pesticide subsidies developed a methodology for preliminary measurement of the economic costs of pesticide resistance and examined the effects of cutting pesticide subsidies. One of the most feasible ways of lessening farmers' dependence on pesticides is integrated pest management (IPM), which uses a combination of natural predators, shifting crops and planting patterns, and specifically targeted pesticides. IPM has been shown to reduce external costs while maintaining crop yields.

The application of environmental economics to the management of water and marine resources is to be examined in a number of sectoral case studies. These will lead into major new areas of work on the environmental impacts of macroeconomic and sectoral policies, as discussed below. Related work on integrated land resource management has also begun, using economic tools to explore the links between land, water, and forest resources.

ENVIRONMENTAL ACCOUNTING. Bank research on environmental accounting is designed to address the environmental shortcomings of the current System of National Accounts, published in 1968. Progress has recently been made in developing a framework for integrating environmental concerns into economic accounting. Eighteen papers in this field are to be published in a single volume, *Toward Improved Accounting for the Environment*.[1] The work has four principal elements: (a) a preliminary framework for integrated environmental and economic accounting; (b) case studies of the application of the framework; (c) a specific focus on mineral depreciation; and (d) valuation methods and other possible conceptual approaches to environmental accounting.

Economywide Policies and the Environment

Along with efforts to incorporate environmental considerations into Bank sector work and project design, the scope of environmental assessment must be expanded to make it relevant to policy-based lending. To do this, the relationship between sectoral and macroeconomic policy reforms (the subject of adjustment lending) and their environmental impacts has to be identified.

CASE STUDIES AND RESEARCH. Bank economic and sector studies were reviewed this year to identify current work that addresses the implications of economic policy for proper management of resources. The role of sectoral and macroeconomic policies in resource management was assessed through a series of country case studies. These studies found two basic patterns that characterize policy-environment linkages in the context of adjustment-related reforms: the unanticipated production and substitution effects that economic reforms have on resource use, and the poverty and environmental degradation associated with inappropriate policies and programs. The next step will be to synthesize the results of the studies and assess the incorporation of environmental components into adjustment operations.

In addition, the Bank has published a major study of the linkages between international trade and the environment (Low 1992). Issues taken up include the use of trade policy in the pursuit of environmental objectives and the relationship of environmental quality to industrial location; competitiveness; economic growth and trade liberalization; the political economy of environmental policymaking; and international cooperation on the environment. While stressing the need for further empirical work on trade and environment issues, the study draws some preliminary policy conclusions. Among them are that trade measures are seldom the optimal means for addressing environmental externalities; that when environmental objectives cannot be addressed adequately in a domestic setting, international cooperation offers better prospects for sound environmental outcomes than do punitive unilateral sanctions; that national differences in environmental regulations have not been a major explanatory factor in the changing international patterns of location of "dirty" industries; and that fast-growing economies with liberal trade policies have experienced less pollution-intensive growth than closed economies.

PUBLIC ECONOMICS. The Bank's overall research program on public economics has been shifting away from the traditional focus on tax policy and toward issues of public expenditure, poverty, and the environment. A major research project on pollution and the choice of policy instruments, initiated last year, assesses the economic costs of different policy instruments—taxes and regulations—used to address local pollution problems. It develops an analytical framework for evaluating alternative measures and applies it to several cases, including those of Indonesia, Mexico, and Poland. The interim results of the project will be synthesized in a "best-practices" paper aimed principally at Bank operational staff.

The case study in Poland is a component of the Bank's continuing assistance in preparing an action program for submission to the Conference of the European Environment Ministers in 1993 (see "Eastern Europe and Central Asia" in chapter 4). The study assesses a range of instruments for achieving acceptable air quality standards in Poland and discusses to some extent the international and global implications of measures to control air pollution—principally sulfur dioxide and carbon dioxide. The second stage of this program will involve more intensive data collection and analysis, focusing especially on the processing of regional data and the impact of macroeconomic reforms and industrial restructuring on air pollution in Poland.

SEMINARS AND PUBLICATIONS. The results of the analytical work and case studies on valuation have been presented in several forums. In particular, analytical tools developed for economic valuation were presented at the Committee of International Development Institutions on the Environment (CIDIE) seminar on environmental economics. This seminar, which the Bank was asked to organize and lead, helped to establish a consensual approach to environmental economics in development work by the members of CIDIE—multilateral banks, bilateral aid agencies, and international development organizations.

Six workshops for Bank staff on environmental-economic techniques, as well as workshops on specific case studies, have been held. These have proved to be the most effective means of incorporating environmental economics into the Bank's operational work. A Bank seminar on the economics of protected areas was presented as part of the World Parks Congress held in Caracas in 1991.

Population, Poverty, and Health

Poverty reduction is the Bank's overarching objective. In his address to UNCED, the president of the Bank urged that more attention be given to the basic needs of the world's poorest:

> Inadequate sanitation affects one-third of the world's population. One billion people are without safe drinking water, and 1.3 billion are exposed to indoor pollution caused by soot and smoke. The livelihoods of hundreds of millions of farmers and forest dwellers are threatened by declining productivity due to soil erosion, deforestation, and other symptoms of poor environmental stewardship. These problems exemplify the link between poverty and the environment. They demand urgent attention. (Preston 1992)

The poor are both victims and agents of environmental damage. Not only do they suffer most from environmental degradation; they also contribute to such degradation because they are forced to live in ecologically fragile zones—marginal agricultural lands and urban slums—and because they lack the resources, property rights, and access to credit necessary for investing in long-term environmental protection. Conversely, since the poor are less able to "escape" environmental problems, they also benefit the most from environmental improvements. Bank research in support of *World Development Report 1992* further stresses that many of the environmental problems faced by developing countries—unsafe water, inadequate sanitation, soil depletion, and indoor pollution from soot and smoke—are closely related to poverty.

World Development Report 1990 outlined a two-pronged strategy for reducing poverty, and the 1991 policy paper *Assistance Strategies to Reduce Poverty* developed ways to put that strategy to work within the Bank. The strategy has two elements. The first is to pursue broadly based economic growth that generates income-earning opportunities for the poor and makes use of the poor's most abundant asset, their labor. The second is to ensure that the poor can take full advantage of these opportunities, by improving their access to education, health care, and other social services. In addition, the strategy emphasizes the need for a safety net for the poorest segments of society.

The recently issued Operational Directive on Poverty Reduction and the "Poverty Reduction Handbook" are intended to guide staff in implementing this strategy. The operational directive provides practical guidelines, while the handbook offers further details, highlighting examples of good practice on the basis of a review of Bank operations and economic and sector work. The new operational directive requires that poverty assessments be prepared for all active borrowers to help in the formulation of country strategies. It notes that "maintaining the environment is critical if gains in poverty reduction are to be sustained and if future increases in poverty are to be avoided."

Research also emphasizes the substantial synergies that exist between alleviating poverty and protecting the environment. Economic activities stimulated by environmental policies—such as agroforestry or improvements in sanitation infrastructure—often employ large numbers of poor people. Targeted social safety nets make it less necessary for the poor to "mine" natural resources during crisis periods. Investments in pollution abatement benefit the poor by improving their health and productivity. Above all, equitable economic growth, coupled with educational and health services, will enable the poor to make environmental investments that are in their own long-term interest. It will also be essential for accelerating demographic transition, since better-off and better-educated couples have fewer children.

One measure of efforts to reduce poverty is the breadth of Bank activities designed to benefit the poor directly. During fiscal 1992 projects were launched to improve the productivity of small farmers, to provide basic education, water supply, and sanitation services, and to reinforce basic infrastructure in regions of concentrated poverty. Specific poverty studies bearing on the environment that are currently under way address the impact of agricultural policies on poor households; improvement of women's access to education, health care, agricultural extension, and credit; and the performance of targeted programs in health, education, and water supply. An ongoing research project examines the impact of urban environmental degradation on slum dwellers and squatters. Related work has been initiated in the Environment Department to identify specific operational issues arising from the linkages between poverty reduction and environmental degradation.

Population Growth and the Poverty Trap

The global population now stands at 5.4 billion and is growing by more than 93 million people a year. Although fertility levels are declining in many parts of the developing world (with the exception of most of Africa), 1 billion people are still being added to the planet every eleven years. The Bank's base case projections indicate that between 1990 and 2030 the world's population will grow by 3.7 billion, stabilizing at 12.5

billion around the middle of the twenty-second century. Two-thirds of this increase will occur by 2050, and 95 percent will take place in the developing world.

As population increases, so does the need for employment, resulting in direct pressure on natural resources. More people produce more wastes, threatening local health conditions and further taxing the earth's assimilative capacity. Traditional land management practices are unable to prevent environmental degradation, and the results are overgrazing, deforestation, depletion of water resources, and loss of natural habitat. As people move to urban areas over the next forty years, cities in developing countries are expected to grow by 160 percent, exacerbating air and water pollution and increasing energy consumption and industrial waste.

The Bank's emphasis on reducing population growth is part of its overall effort to address environmental concerns, attack poverty, and spur economic growth. The diverse nature of population projects reflects the effort not only to address the unmet need for contraception that exists in most countries but also to stimulate the demand for family planning that derives from better infant and maternal health and from improvements in women's status. Thus, programs that once provided only family planning services are now incorporating maternal and child health care, nutrition interventions, health and education, and income-generating activities for women.

Bank lending for population, health, and nutrition activities has grown from $305 million in 1988 to nearly $1 billion in fiscal 1992. This year $103 million was lent specifically for population, and the amount is expected to increase to about $250 million in fiscal 1993.

The Bank's new population adviser will provide leadership for the institution and will act as chief spokesperson for the Bank on population issues. The adviser will work to improve the effectiveness of Bank lending operations, sector work, and policy and research activities, with a view to reducing rapid population growth and high fertility and incorporating demographic considerations into development planning in general. To this end, the adviser will counsel senior management on the Bank's population strategy and will work to ensure the technical quality of the Bank's population activities.

Health

In many parts of the developing world, ill health is linked to poverty and a degraded environment. An estimated 1.7 billion people still lack access to proper sanitation services, and hundreds of millions of the rural poor have no access to clean water.

Two recent or forthcoming publications by the Bank highlight environmental health issues. *Disease Priorities in Developing Countries,*[2] a review of priorities in the health sector, assesses the public health significance of major diseases in the developing world and the cost-effectiveness of available interventions. *The Health of Adults in the Developing World* (Feachem and others 1992) notes that new sources of pollution of water, food, and air are often created by industrialization and economic development and calls for preventive approaches that can decrease the associated health risks.

In the coming year the Bank will address environmental health issues in *World Development Report 1993*. The report, which will focus on human health in the developing world, will include a chapter on behavioral, social, and environmental interventions and will discuss ways of enhancing environmental quality to improve health conditions.

Energy, Industry, and Urbanization

Unless current energy and industrial policies are reconsidered, pollution from fossil fuel generation of electric power will rise more than ten times in the next forty years; vehicle emissions will increase five times, as will industrial emissions and waste. As developing countries begin to "catch up" with the levels of energy consumption and industrial production of the industrial world, their increasing consumption of commercial energy will pose particularly urgent environmental problems. Bank research suggests that without altered policies, developing country consumption of commercial energy will soon dominate energy markets worldwide. The Bank remains committed to promoting ways for developing countries to reduce pollution from energy use, even as output and demand expand.

Energy Use and Efficiency

Bank loans for the energy sector have increased substantially over the past two decades. Since 1979 at least thirty-five projects have been entirely devoted to energy efficiency. These include projects designed to improve efficiency in petroleum refineries and in a range of manufacturing industries: fertilizers (Yugoslavia), pulp and paper (Turkey), textiles (Philippines and Turkey), cement (India), and metals (Egypt and Guyana).

ELECTRIC POWER. The Bank has sought to promote improvements in energy efficiency in a variety of ways. For example, it has pushed programs to retrofit old power plants, strengthen and upgrade electric power transmission and distribution systems, and establish energy audits and national institutions to encourage energy efficiency. Increasingly, the Bank is becoming less involved in the direct transfer of resources to power sectors in developing countries; instead, it is helping these countries put in place systems that encourage the efficient use of power sector resources.

A policy paper, "The Bank's Role in the Electric Power Sector," examines the experiences of industrial and borrower countries in developing their own power sectors and discusses specific approaches the Bank should pursue to help countries develop a self-sustaining power sector. It recommends, first, that all power sector loans be made within a proper legal framework and transparent regulatory process. Second, where market forces are lacking, public and private sectors are weak, and capital markets are undeveloped, electric power services should be brought in or upgraded by other countries. Third, the Bank should pursue the commercialization and corporatization of developing country power utilities. Fourth, Bank lending for electric power should concentrate on those countries with a clear commitment to improving sector performance. Finally, in order to encourage private investment in the power sector, the Bank should use some of its own financial resources to underwrite programs that facilitate the involvement of private investors.

ENERGY EFFICIENCY. The issue of energy efficiency is becoming more salient in many developing countries as a result of several forces: a rapidly growing demand for energy, significant constraints on available energy financing, increased pressure to sustain the environment, poor energy performance and more discerning consumers, and a reappraisal of the roles of government and of the public and private sectors in development. Bank research emphasizes the need to improve energy efficiency through institutional reform and the elimination of energy subsidies (which now amount to more than $150 billion a year in developing countries). This kind of strategy—in combination with the use of environmental taxes and regulations as an incentive for the energy industry and its consumers to adopt cleaner fuels, such as natural gas, and clean fuel technologies, such as controls on particulate emissions—can reduce pollution dramatically while leading to large cost savings in energy production and use.

In fiscal 1992 a comprehensive review of the potential for increased energy efficiency ("Energy Efficiency and Conservation in the Developing World: The World Bank's Role") was prepared as part of the Bank's effort to formulate a strategy for promoting energy efficiency. The paper argues that efforts to address countrywide policy and institutional issues are the most important means for achieving improvements in energy efficiency. Integrated energy strategies being proposed involve the following elements: (a) energy prices should reflect real supply costs, including pollution abatement costs; (b) barriers to the development of competitive energy markets should be eliminated; (c) institutional and regulatory structures should become more decentralized and transparent; and (d) measures should be implemented to facilitate technology transfer and greater energy efficiency in the transport sector.

Such strategies can have substantial economic impacts in developing countries because of the possibilities for delaying capital-intensive investments in energy supply and the potential for fuel savings. Several studies estimate that even in the short term, a savings of 20 to 25 percent of energy consumed by the existing capital stock could be achieved in developing countries without sacrificing the economic benefits of energy use. Over the longer term, as investments are made in new capital equipment, larger energy savings are possible, on the order of 30 to 60 percent over what is possible with current equipment.

The review concludes that Bank strategy should be organized around a four-point program: (a) energy efficiency issues should be addressed earlier and should be more thoroughly integrated into the Bank's country policy dialogue; (b) the Bank should be more selective in lending to energy supply institutions; (c) efforts to improve intermediation in energy and industry markets in developing countries should be identified, supported, and given high-level visibility within the borrower country in order to reduce the higher costs of information, management, technology, and financing transactions; and (d) transfer of energy-saving and pollution abatement technology should receive more attention in Bank sector and project work.

COMMERCIAL ENERGY EFFICIENCY AND THE ENVIRONMENT. A similar research effort on commercial energy efficiency and the environment concluded that higher priority should be given to greater energy efficiency in the developing world (including Central and Eastern Europe). Of particular benefit would be the elimination or reduction of energy pricing distortions, which offers a cost-effective means of mitigating the harmful environmental consequences of growing energy consumption.

There are several advantages to such a strategy. Energy efficiency requires measures that ultimately strengthen the economy and are cost-effective. It also conserves supplies of nonrenewable fuels, especially fossil fuels, and encourages appropriate fuel substitution and switching. Furthermore, energy efficiency addresses local and national energy problems as well as regional, transnational, and global issues of climate change.

The research also found that any strategy for making energy production and use more efficient must rely more extensively on markets that are allowed to function with less government interference. In this context, it is essential to remove energy subsidies and pursue key macroeconomic and structural reforms. It is also important that industrial countries facilitate improvements in energy efficiency in the developing world through technology transfer, commercial mechanisms—such as partnerships and licensing arrangements—and support for research and development.

Energy Sector Management Assistance Program

The joint UNDP–World Bank Energy Sector Management Assistance Programme (ESMAP), established in 1983, is a technical assistance program that promotes more efficient use of energy in developing countries. The program operates in about thirty countries, helping recipient governments design a relevant and coherent set of energy policies that address environmental issues linked to the energy sector. ESMAP also provides technical assistance, augmenting local capabilities and capacities to manage resources.

ESMAP has provided valuable technical assistance and training this year in a number of countries: energy conservation and strategy development in Pakistan; power system planning in Kenya and Tanzania; natural gas sector planning in Mozambique; and rural energy planning in China and Zimbabwe. ESMAP will continue to incorporate technical assistance and capacity-building elements into virtually all its country programs.

In many cases, energy-importing developing countries use energy inefficiently and have rudimentary electricity grids. Over the next few years ESMAP will look at the environmental implications of a country's energy mix. Such assessments are instrumental in fashioning national energy strategies to meet development goals without causing further environmental deterioration. They are also vital in assisting countries to meet their obligations under the Climate Change Convention concluded at UNCED.

Industrial Pollution

In 1984 and 1988 the Bank issued guidelines for abatement measures aimed at curbing industrial pollution. These guidelines, however, omitted a number of key sectors such as thermal power stations and sewage treatment plants and did not address the management, treatment, and disposal of hazardous wastes. Moreover, most remedial measures were based on "end of the pipe" treatment technologies and disposal concepts. Little attention was paid to waste reduction.

Over the past year the Bank has been working to remedy these oversights by revising or updating approximately eighty-five industrial pollution guidelines for various industrial sectors and pollutants. The revised guidelines will emphasize techniques for preventing pollution and minimizing waste, including cleaner processes and conservation of resources. The four "Rs"—reduction, reuse, recycling, and recovery—will receive considerable attention in new lending programs. Hazardous waste management will focus on long-term monitoring and on safer disposal techniques in an effort to minimize harmful environmental impacts.

Also under development this year was an important participatory method of prioritizing strategies for controlling urban industrial pollution. It examines emissions to air, water, and land associated with industrial activity and traffic and simulates the concentration and emission patterns of pollutants, allowing the effects of different pollution control measures to be evaluated and ranked according to their relative costs and associated health risks. Information on the various alternatives puts community representatives and planners in a better position to negotiate a preferred pollution control scenario. The software package is being developed for operational applications on a standard personal computer.

Further work was done on the creation and diffusion of industrial environmental technologies by the Environmental Technology Project. The study uses data on patents in various environmental fields, together with related information on equipment flows, domestic production, regulations, and pollution indices. It analyzes two sets of issues: the incentives to create pollution control technologies or environmentally friendly technologies, and the diffusion of such environmental technologies to developing countries. The second set of issues encompasses the range of approaches developing countries may employ to obtain these technologies.

The prototype development of the Industrial Pollution Projection System (IPPS) was completed this year in collaboration with the United Nations Industrial Development Organization (UNIDO), the U.S. Census Bureau, and the U.S. Environmental Protection Agency. This new information system is designed to construct comprehensive profiles of industrial pollution for countries, regions, urban areas, or proposed projects. It is intended for use by developing countries that lack reliable information about their own industrial pollution problems.

The IPPS covers hundreds of pollutants, all operating technologies, and approximately 1,500 product categories. It can project emissions of industrial air and water pollutants, solid waste, greenhouse gases, and ozone-depleting compounds separately and incorporates all known risk factors for toxic and ecotoxic effects, carcinogenic risk, and heavy metal buildup.

Estimates made by the IPPS have already been used in a variety of Bank projects. The Indonesian Environmental Management Study includes an industrial pollution control strategy that analyzes the impact of past policies on industrial pollution levels and forecasts the consequences of various alternative strategies for future industrial development. The IPPS has also been used to estimate industrial pollution for the Asia Environment Report, pollution damage estimates for Mexico, and pollution projections for Brazil.

Urbanization and the "Brown Agenda"

The immediate and most critical environmental problems facing cities in the developing world have been collectively dubbed the "brown agenda"—lack of safe water supply, sanitation, and drainage; inadequate management of solid and hazardous wastes; uncontrolled emissions from factories, vehicles, and low-grade domestic fuels; accidents linked to congestion and overcrowding; and the occupation and degradation of environmentally sensitive areas. The costs of these problems fall most heavily on current generations, particularly the urban poor, who pay for them in chronic ill health, lower productivity, and reduced income and quality of life.

The environmental problems of urban wastes and pollution are inextricably linked to poverty and productivity as well as to broader macroeconomic performance. Furthermore, resolving "brown" issues in cities has crucial implications for the resolution of many "green" problems (management and use of natural resources) beyond urban boundaries. For example, a significant reduction of carbon dioxide emissions at the global level requires energy-efficient technologies and conservation measures in urban areas. Each city has its own mix of problems, requiring a specific and dynamic blend of curative and preventive solutions.

The environmental component of the Urban Management Program (UMP)—a UNDP-funded program jointly executed by the World Bank and UNCHS-Habitat (United Nations Center for Human Settlements)—focuses on this "brown agenda." The program conducts research, promotes appropriate policies, and provides technical assistance to developing countries to improve urban environmental management. Emphasizing local participation and consultation, the UMP establishes partnerships with regional, national, and global support networks for applied research and for the dissemination of information on best practices and promising alternative management strategies.

The first phase of the UMP, involving research, background studies, and fieldwork on a wide range of issues, seeks to identify broad environmental management strategies for dealing with critical urban environmental problems. The chief product of this effort will be a report on environmental strategies for cities, which aims to develop an analytical framework for environmental planning and for understanding urban environmental problems and formulating responses. The framework focuses on the underlying causes of environmental degradation in cities; the needed policies, instruments, and institutional reforms; and a participatory environmental planning and management process. The anticipated outcome of the process is an investment program to implement urban environmental management projects, as well as policy reforms and institutional arrangements.

During the past fiscal year considerable background research was completed for the framework paper: priorities for urban waste management and pollution control; the local management of wastes from small-scale and cottage industries; economic valuation of environmental problems, with an emphasis on Asian cities; public and private sector management approaches; the environmental dimensions of urban land management; the application of urban environmental indicators for testing in city case studies; a review of the literature on the relative health impacts of environmental problems in urban areas; and the application of remote sensing and Geographic Information Systems (GIS) to urban environmental planning.

The UMP also completed environmental profiles in six developing country cities (Accra, Jakarta, Katowice, São Paulo, Tianjin, and Tunis) and in the Singrauli region of India. The profiles will enable these cities to develop a viable urban environmental management strategy (see box 5-1).

In the second phase of the program, the emphasis of the environmental component will shift from global research to country and city-level activities in an effort to raise public awareness and obtain political commitment for the development of environmental strategies and action plans.

During fiscal 1992 the UMP drew on and contributed to other Bank environmental efforts such as the Metropolitan Environmental Improvement Program, *World Development Report 1992*, and urban environmental sector work and lending and was active in defining an urban agenda of environmental concerns for UNCED. The program also supported other international efforts such as the Toronto Conference on World Cities and the Environment in October 1991 and the World Urban Forum held in Curitiba, Brazil, prior to UNCED.

Box 5-1. Participating in the Urban Environment

A project conducted by the Urban Management Program and a consortium of Canadian groups identified environmental agendas in five cities: Accra (Ghana), Jakarta (Indonesia), Katowice (Poland), São Paulo (Brazil), and Toronto (Canada). In each city a three-step process was used to develop an understanding of environmental priorities. An urban environmental questionnaire was designed to generate information on important indicators such as land use; air, water, and noise pollution; wastes; transport; and energy use. In order to note the conditions, factors, and trends that influence environmental quality in these cities, an environmental profile was prepared by local experts. In addition, the results of the questionnaires were elaborated during consultations with citizens in each city, culminating in an "environmental town meeting."

This experience resulted in a consensus on one or more environmental priorities in each city. In Accra waste disposal and sanitation was considered the highest priority. In Jakarta, inadequate waste management was cited as the most important issue, followed by deteriorating air and water quality, substandard housing, inadequate transport, and lack of sufficient green space. The top three concerns in Katowice were to increase public awareness about ecology and health problems caused by pollution, restructure industrial activity to reduce negative environmental impacts, and improve public access to environmental information and decisionmaking. In São Paulo five issues topped the urban environmental agenda: negative environmental impacts from squatter settlements and slums; inadequate land-use and green-space policies; the links between natural resources, public health, and basic sanitation; energy-transport-pollution linkages; and popular participation in environmental management.

The principal conclusions were that although there is no uniform environmental agenda for cities in the developing world, there are specific local environmental concerns which are distinct from those considered to be part of the global environmental agenda. Where local and global environmental issues overlap, the reasons for concern are not always the same. For example, local people seemed to be concerned about green spaces for reasons of quality of life and health, not because of longer-term global consequences such as climate change and loss of biodiversity.

Transport

In cooperation with the UNEP, the Bank has prepared a comprehensive report on automotive air pollution. The report analyses options for control of vehicle emissions in the light of technological, economic, and institutional constraints, highlighting the contribution of motor vehicles to the deterioration of urban air quality in developing countries. It assesses the main economic instruments that can be used to facilitate measures to control motor vehicle emissions and discusses the institutional requirements for implementing emission control strategies in countries at vastly different levels of development. A sector study for Mexico City specifically addresses the issue of vehicle-related air pollution: a similar study is being undertaken for Bangkok.

In order to raise the awareness of Bank staff concerning the provisions of the Protocol on Prevention of Pollution from Ships (MARPOL), a brief technical policy note was drafted. This note will be used to promote greater recognition of the benefits of implementing MARPOL and will help ensure that the objectives of the protocol are taken into account when port projects are prepared by the Bank.

A practical handbook on environmental road design is also in preparation. It will focus on the impact of new road projects on the environment, address different types of environmental impacts, and look at specific aspects related to road construction and maintenance. Aimed at national highway directorates and design and project managers, the manual will deal with the organization of relevant environmental units and methods and will offer practical recommendations for different types of impact and some basic terms of reference for carrying out studies, based on broad international experience.

Major policy and research work is planned in the coming year to address broader questions of urban and mass transport in developing countries. In addition, some regional activities are shifting attention toward mass transit, cleaner fuels, and efforts to improve traffic flows.

Where climate and terrain are appropriate, the Bank has promoted the use of nonmotorized vehicles. Several pilot studies and projects have been instituted: in China the Bank has financed the construction of bicycle paths in the central areas of Tianjin and Shanghai, and in Ghana the use of nonmotorized vehicles in rural areas has been promoted. Several seminars have been organized to familiarize Bank staff with the issue of nonmotorized forms of transport, and the IBRD and the Inter-American Development Bank (IDB) are preparing a joint technical paper on the subject.

Water Pollution, Scarcity, and Management

Water is a natural resource crucial for economic development. Yet in many places around the world, the capacity of water resources is being pushed to dangerous extremes. Water scarcity no longer refers to shortages alone; it also applies to situations in which water is abundant but

94

pollution forecloses beneficial uses. Formidable challenges face the sustainable management of water resources: rapid population growth and increasing agricultural and urban demands for water, failing water quality and water pollution; health impacts; depletion of groundwater; and conflict over shared resources.

An integrated approach to water management is essential if a crisis is to be avoided in water-short countries over the next decade. The Bank is now developing explicit procedures for addressing intersectoral water resource issues comprehensively.

Water Policy

A policy paper is being prepared to work out an integrated approach to the development and management of water resources. This paper will take account of the various uses of water, such as urban consumption, irrigation, and industry, with the aim of ensuring their coordination and their compatibility with national objectives and with efficient allocation of resources. Significant attention will be given to the environmental aspects of the management of water resources. Issues related to wetlands, soil erosion in watersheds, and water pollution caused by domestic, industrial, and agricultural uses will be highlighted.

Water Supply and Sanitation

Between 1966 and 1992 the Bank lent more than $18 billion for irrigation and drainage projects and another $13 billion for water supply and sewerage. In fiscal 1992 Bank lending for water supply and sanitation projects amounted to more than $900 million and funded efforts in ten countries. Two projects—one for international waters and another for river and coastal waters—are designed specifically to reduce water pollution by means of improved treatment of wastes.

In addition, the Bank played a major role in the International Conference on Water and the Environment, held in Dublin in January 1992 as part of the preparations for UNCED. The conference's final statement on the importance of water to sustainable development observed:

Scarcity and misuse of fresh water pose a serious and growing threat to sustainable development and protection of the environment. Human health and welfare, food security, industrial development, and the ecosystems on which they depend, are all at risk, unless water and land resources are managed more effectively in the present decade and beyond than they have been in the past.

Improving basic water and sanitation services is an important first step in alleviating poverty, protecting the environment, and promoting human development. The UNDP–World Bank Water and Sanitation Program has been addressing these issues since the beginning of the International Drinking Water and Sanitation Decade of the 1980s. Working to expand sustainable water and sanitation services to poor communities, the joint program helps developing countries provide potable water, sanitation services, and waste management to low-income communities in rural and urban areas.

WATER RESOURCES MANAGEMENT. This past year the Operations Evaluation Department (OED) reviewed the Bank's experience in the urban water supply and sanitation sector between 1967 and 1989. Reporting on 120 projects, the study concluded that although the Bank and its borrowers have successfully delivered potable water to millions of urban dwellers, they were less successful in addressing waste disposal and sanitation problems. Shortcomings were also evident in achieving institutional development targets and making utilities financially viable. Operation and maintenance, critical elements for the sustainability of project benefits, also received inadequate attention.

On the basis of these studies, the OED recommended, among other things, careful and comprehensive assessment of water resources before project design and implementation; better coordination of water agencies; integration of drainage networks into the design of any irrigation project, and inclusion of antierosion measures and afforestation in the design of reservoir catchment areas. The OED also called on the Bank to analyze operational and maintenance capacities and to refrain from making new investments until a borrower's institutional capacities are considered adequate.

INTEGRATED ECOLOGICAL MANAGEMENT OF RIVER BASINS. As part of its reevaluation of water projects, the Bank is developing an approach designed to preserve the integrity of river basin ecosystems. River basins are essential for maintaining the earth's life support systems; they transport nutrients to coastal waters, house biodiversity, help regulate regional climate, and provide water for irrigated agriculture.

Mounting population pressures, poorly conceived irrigation and hydropower projects, inadequate waste treatment, and generally poor land and water management practices have contributed to the overexploitation and misuse of river basin water resources. In many developing countries the resulting scarcity and deteriorating quality of water not only increase the costs of water and energy supply but also threaten to undermine further economic development.

The Bank's program ot integrated environmental management will include (a) development of a conceptual and methodological framework for project preparation and appraisal; (b) development of criteria and guidelines for environmental assessment procedures; and (c) identification of investment opportunities under Bank, GEF, and other funding schemes at the country and regional levels.

A review of Bank experience in river basin management, focusing on regional impact assessment, institutional strengthening, and project and program design, is already under way. The case studies, drawn from Bank experience, will identify key issues and lessons learned.

Marine and Coastal Issues

Coral reefs, mangroves, seagrass beds, salt marshes, and estuaries are among the world's most productive and most endangered ecosystems. They provide vital breeding grounds and habitats for a wide variety of fish and shellfish, shelter coasts from the ravages of storms, and inhibit erosion. But they have been disappearing at alarming rates. Of the world's 600,000 square kilometers of coral reefs, for example, only half are thought to be in good condition (that is, with more than 50 percent live coral cover). Only a tiny fraction of the world's coastal wetlands remains intact.

Few inventories of marine biodiversity have been carried out, and most surveys are limited to specific areas. In many regions the extent to which these highly fecund life support systems have been damaged is simply not known.

Mapping Marine Biodiversity

To generate more comprehensive data on the state of marine biodiversity, the Bank, in collaboration with the World Conservation Union (IUCN), is heading a global research effort to map out areas rich in marine life. A representative system of protected marine areas would constitute a major building block in the Bank's marine biodiversity activities under the GEF. For purposes of organization and analysis, the world has been divided into thirteen regions, each of which will be surveyed for its number and diversity of marine species. In addition to mapping marine biodiversity, this exercise will generate a valuable pool of information on the current state of marine parks and protected areas and will identify priority areas for the conservation of marine biodiversity.

The data and information from the survey will be used to identify those areas in need of immediate protection or further financing. The exercise will also determine which areas are merely "paper parks" whose primary function—serving as marine reserves—has been undermined by lack of management plans, personnel, or funds. Where important ecosystems are found to be under threat, they can be given higher priority for conservation initiatives.

One case study, that of the Bonaire Marine Park in the Netherlands Antilles, has the potential to serve as a management model for marine protected areas in the Caribbean and elsewhere. The island of Bonaire found that with sound management of the park, it was able to maintain a marine-based tourist economy without damaging the resources on which it depends. The cost of maintaining the park—$150,000 a year—is easily recouped by the $10 diving and snorkeling fees charged to tourists. Overall, marine-based tourism generates a gross revenue for Bonaire of $21 million a year, about half the island's total GDP.

Coastal Zone Management

Nearly 70 percent of the world's population lives on or within 80 kilometers of a seacoast. Urban centers, in particular, seem to be growing faster in coastal areas than elsewhere. In many countries, both industrial and developing, inappropriate land use practices are overtaxing coastal ecosystems, degrading natural resources, and compounding environmental problems.

The Bank's special initiative on coastal zone management addresses the environmental effects of nonsustainable coastal land use, focusing on the development of practical and effective procedures for the management of coastal ecosystems. The initiative has included case studies and training for Bank staff. For example, a one-day training workshop on integrated coastal zone management, held in collaboration with the Bank's Training Division, presented case studies on sustainable utilization of coastal and near-shore marine resources.

Several new initiatives are being launched within the Bank, including the Caribbean-Wide Marine Program. An ongoing case study of urban coastal zone management in Brazil is expected to produce additional results to help address the waste disposal and related problems of densely populated metropolitan areas. This operationally oriented study will yield management recommendations applicable in many developing countries.

Future work on coastal zone management will include an inventory and assessment of upcoming Bank-supported projects in coastal zones, especially those that may have significant impacts on coastal resources; development of new directives and guidelines to support Bank operational activities in coastal zones, including technical support for project design and implementation; and development of special guidelines for the protection of historical and archaeological sites from development activities in coastal areas.

The main activities planned for the second phase of the initiative include the integration of coastal zone planning into environmental action plans, support for the Bank's regional Technical Departments in implementing EAP guidelines and procedures, and the strengthening of planning capacities and local coastal management capabilities in borrowing countries.

Agriculture and Forestry

Forest Policy

Early in the fiscal year, the release of the forest sector policy paper served to clarify the Bank's commitment to strengthening work in the sector. The policy paper identifies two key challenges: to slow the alarmingly rapid rates of deforestation, especially (although not exclusively) in tropical moist forests, and to ensure adequate planting of new trees to meet the rapidly growing demand for fuelwood in developing countries. Bank objectives include support for international efforts and legal instruments to promote forest conservation; assistance to governments with policy reform and institutional strengthening; creation of additional forest resources; and support for initiatives to preserve intact forest areas.

To these ends, the Bank states explicitly that it will not, under any circumstances, finance commercial logging in primary moist tropical forests. In addition, infrastructural projects that might lead to the loss of primary forests will be subject to rigorous environmental assessment. Forest sector activities will be linked more closely to country economic and sector work.

Lending operations in the forest sector will distinguish between projects that are environmentally protective or are oriented toward small farmers and all other forestry operations. Whereas the former will be considered on the basis of their economic, social, and environmental merits, the latter will be conditional on governmental commitment to sustainable and conservation-oriented forestry.

Land Degradation and Sustainable Agriculture

A background paper for *World Development Report 1992*, "Global Food—Resources and Prospects for the Major Cereals," explored the circumstances under which the global agricultural system may be able to satisfy the growing demand for certain major food crops to 2030. The study reviewed the quantity and quality of resources that can be mobilized,

particularly those relating to land, water, plant genetic resourc
change, and knowledge about agricultural production syste:
   The study finds that by 2030 global grain consumption w.. _
97 percent greater than in the past few years and that 91 percent of this
growth will be in developing countries. The only economically and
environmentally feasible means of meeting this demand is to boost crop
yields on existing agricultural land. This will require appropriate investment, particularly in agricultural research. The Bank has long been
involved in agricultural research through its support for the Consultative Group on International Agricultural Research (CGIAR), the Special
Program for African Agricultural Research (SPAAR), and the improvement of national agricultural research systems.

LAND DEGRADATION. An expert meeting jointly sponsored by the Bank's
Agriculture and Environment departments in early fiscal 1992 addressed issues of land degradation and management and noted the lack
of information on soil conservation programs and the relative ineffec-
tiveness of these programs. As a result, a series of studies of the performance of soil conservation programs in Central America (involving the
construction of terraces and many other structural or agronomic measures) is being undertaken with the Centre Agronómico Tropical de
Investigación y Enseñanza (CATIE). Preliminary results caution against
focusing programs around a single technology, since the consequent
disruption of traditional cultivation methods can reduce yields both in
absolute terms and in relation to the results achieved through the incremental adoption of small-scale cultivation technologies such as contour
plowing and planting, tree lines to cut down on erosion, and modified
crop rotation and planting patterns.
   Another study, carried out with the Overseas Development Institute in London, is examining the experience of a semiarid district in
Kenya where, despite a doubling of agricultural productivity per
capita and a fivefold increase in population, soil degradation has been
significantly reduced over the past two decades. Where initial government efforts to promote narrow-based terraces met with mixed
results, bench terracing was later independently and successfully
adopted by farmers, partly in response to expanded market access,
particularly for cash crops. The study stresses the importance of
market outlets in providing the widest possible range of economically
and technically viable land use options, permitting the land user to
devise a sustainable system and modify it as economic and social
circumstances change. The study emphasized that this adoption process is integral to the process of agricultural innovation and should
not be addressed separately.

DRYLAND MANAGEMENT. Because of a complex and variable combination of social, institutional, and technical deficiencies in project and program design, few rangeland management projects have had a discernable impact on the way rangeland is generally used. Recent Bank work on the biology of rangelands and herbivores, particularly in Africa, has called into question the range management techniques promoted in recent decades and the theoretical assumptions underpinning them. Bank studies suggest a need to allow—or even prompt—free herd movement so as to exploit fully the ecological heterogeneity of these dry rangelands and arrive at sustainable range management systems. In addition, these studies suggest that earlier concerns about degradation of rangelands and "overstocking" may have been overstated and that pastoralists should not necessarily be discouraged from stocking at higher levels. A major challenge, therefore, will be to design pastoral organizations and land tenure systems that can accommodate the flexibility required for sustainable rangeland systems.

Other studies have examined the operational implications of more opportunistic strategies. They include an analysis of recent studies of rangeland ecology and their implications for the management of communal rangeland areas, and modeling work on optimal resource utilization in an ecological system of this type and on the implications of modifications in the relevant economic policy variables.

SUSTAINABLE AGRICULTURE. To date, agricultural research has tended to address land management as a subsidiary issue. The Bank is seeking to correct this imbalance by developing strategies for integrated land resource management, with particular emphasis on environmentally sensitive areas such as humid tropical forests and drylands. Coincident with the CGIAR's annual International Centers' Week, the Bank organized a meeting of representatives of International Agricultural Research Centers (IARCs) to examine how closer collaboration between the Bank and the IARCs could be developed. Discussions on this topic focused, in particular, on the CGIAR's revised mandate to increase research activities relating directly to environmental aspects of land use, especially soil management and conservation. A meeting of IARC social scientists, planned for August 1992, will explore, among other issues, the possibility of establishing a research network in this area.

RENEWABLE RESOURCE MANAGEMENT IN AGRICULTURE. This year the OED initiated an agricultural management review of Nepal which argues for careful assessment of macroeconomic instruments, such as structural adjustment lending, and for public investment and expenditure reviews. In particular, the review recommends that the definitions of economic growth and comparative advantage be modified to incorporate an expanded notion of opportunity costs and economic pricing. Efforts to formulate macroeconomic strategy and sectoral adjustment policies should be consolidated as much as possible to reduce the risk of mutual contradiction. The OED review also argues for modification of lending instruments in order to dissuade donors from allocating scarce resources for short-term development gains.

Social and Cultural Issues

Many of the most pressing environmental questions are concerned not with natural resources themselves, but with their management, which is largely an institutional and social matter. The *participation of all relevant social actors*, local and distant, in sound environmental management strategies is the social cornerstone needed at the basis of every environmental policy and program. Therefore, strategies for sustainable use of natural resources must be predicated on a sound understanding of the social groups that use them directly, and of the other groups that may benefit from their services. As *World Development Report 1992* observes, building on the positive links between income growth and the environment, while removing the negative connections between them, requires the involvement of people in decisions about how resources will be used.

Because social concerns permeate environmental issues in development, much of the policy and research on social and cultural issues cross-cuts many development programs in all sectors and in all regional sectoral divisions. The increasingly clear linkages between the Bank's work on environment and its support for poverty reduction, strengthening of grass-roots institutions, and human development indicate that the role of social analysis in the Bank will continue to grow.

Fiscal 1992 saw a substantial strengthening of the Bank's ability to address social issues. A senior adviser for sociology and social policy joined the Environment Department, and topics such as resettlement, indigenous people, and local participation have become a larger part of the department's efforts. A new staff training course on social analysis was offered for Bank task managers, and it will become a regular part of the Bank's staff development program.

Social Research on "Putting People First"

An important outcome of the Bank's social and environmental research and operational work during fiscal 1992 was the publication of a substantially revised and enlarged edition of *Putting People First: Sociological Variables in Rural Development* (Cernea 1991). The book contains contributions by both applied and academic specialists showing new ways in which social science can improve development programs. New chapters and field material were added on such issues as afforestation, involuntary resettlement, better approaches to rangeland management and to water husbandry by water users' associations, and participatory assessment procedures. Independent research on common-property resource management led to a study (Jodha 1992) that provides a comprehensive, empirical analysis of the links between land and trees under common property regimes and the survival strategies of the rural poor in India. Work in support of *World Development Report 1992* by Guggenheim and Koch-Weser (1992) highlighted examples of successful local participation in Bank-supported projects. Case studies of Mexico's agricultural and energy development programs analyzed the institutional and methodological reforms that attempt to "scale up" community participation approaches for broader application. The use of case studies to share positive experiences with participation will continue over the coming year.

Gender Issues, Women, and the Environment

While strong emphasis is put on the central role of people in development and environmental management, particular attention is being paid to gender issues and to the role of specific social groups, primarily that of women. Women contribute more than half of all the food grown every year in the developing world and shoulder the main responsibility for finding and using fuelwood and water. Rural women, in particular, are de facto managers of the natural resources around them—soils, forests, and water—yet they often have little or no control over the means for managing these resources.

In many areas of the developing world, deforestation and environmental degradation caused by population pressures increase the time women spend collecting wood and water. These tasks reduce the time they can devote to agricultural activities, with adverse impacts on household incomes. Often these time-intensive tasks are delegated to children, usually girls, who then miss school. Population pressure on a fragile resource base makes it more difficult for women to provide fuel and water to their families and, in turn, may increase their desire to have more children to help with these tasks. Decreased school attendance for girls has serious implications for future reductions in fertility and for increased pressure on the environment.

Research carried out in the past year suggests that investment in education—especially for girls—is the single most important way of breaking the cycle of poverty, population growth, and environmental degradation. Women with more eduction have access to a wider variety of jobs; educated farmers produce more, earn more, and take better care of the land; educated women have smaller, healthier, and better-educated families. One of the best ways of reducing fertility is to expand women's education while providing greater access to family planning. Because education does so much to ease poverty and slow population growth, it is one of the best environmental policies a country can pursue.

In recognition of these interactions and the fundamental role women play as resource managers, an informal Bank Working Group on Women and the Environment has been meeting periodically since the 1991 Global Assembly for Women and the Environment. Among the group's main objectives is dissemination of information on how women's issues can be incorporated into Bank environmental and development programs and projects. Recent topics addressed by the group have included rural water supply, solid waste management, environmental assessment, and social forestry.

WOMEN IN AGRICULTURE. In order to better understand the important role women play in food production, the Bank has undertaken, with UNDP assistance, a study of women as food producers and land managers in Africa. This study involves case studies in Burkina Faso, Kenya, Nigeria, and Zambia. The case studies highlight the problems women face as food producers and their struggle for recognition as farmers. In particular, they illustrate that women have fewer economic opportunities and less access to information and credit than men. Women must also cope with the health problems caused by frequent pregnancies.

The cases also identify ways of overcoming these problems, such as helping women manage natural resources through community action and gearing agricultural extension more to the needs of women. The Women in Agriculture (WIA) program in Nigeria has accomplished this, through what started as a pilot program and now operates on a national level. During the fiscal year the WIA program supported the management of community woodlots, particularly in northern Nigeria, where desertification is an increasingly serious problem. The program has been successful because it has strong government support, especially in the Agriculture Ministry; it incurs minimum additional costs, since most of the female agents are retrained home economics staff already on the government's payroll; it is integrated into the main extension service and so has not become marginalized; and it benefits from Bank support.

OTHER STUDIES. Another Bank study in Africa examines the connection between women's familial and social roles, the constraints and disincentives women face in their social and economic environment, and the degradation of natural resources. The second phase will review the past twelve years of Bank experience in Sub-Saharan Africa, linking gender and environmental issues. The last phase will focus on developing materials for in-house training of Bank task managers to further the integration of gender and environment issues into development work.

In addition, a nearly complete Bank study examines the role of gender in the demand for water and sanitation services, how inadequate infrastructure and services affect women and their labor time, and the additional costs associated with poorly provided public services. In South Asia a review of women's issues resulted in a strategy to incorporate gender into urban water supply projects and policies. This year a comprehensive study examined demographic, agricultural, and environmental problems in Sub-Saharan Africa, with attention to the role of women as managers of natural resources (see box 4-2).

LOOKING AHEAD. As the Bank's work on gender continues to grow, a number of issues are becoming clear for the decade of the 1990s:

- Women's experience as the principal managers of natural resources needs to be better utilized in the identification and implementation of Bank projects.
- Greater attention needs to be given to women's critical role in water supply, sanitation, disposal of solid wastes, forestry and energy.
- Both men and women need enhanced and appropriate education and training in environmental management.
- More recognition should be given to the important links between poverty and environmental degradation, fertility levels, and women's access to family planning and maternal and child health care services in formulating development strategies.

Resettlement Programs

Involuntary resettlement is often an unavoidable consequence of development projects. Although resettlement is commonly associated with large projects for construction of dams and reservoirs for energy and irrigation, in fact it also arises in areas as diverse as potable water supply projects, wildlife protection activities, and projects to improve urban housing, sanitation, and transport.

Through its resettlement policy (first articulated in 1980) and an active research program, the Bank has sought to improve the design and implementation of involuntary resettlement programs. In 1986 a Bank-wide corrective action exercise was initiated to address the policy, institutional, financial, and social issues associated with involuntary resettlement. Additional guidelines were produced in 1986 and 1988, and the Bank's policy was revised and strengthened in 1990. During the 1980s staff specialized in resettlement were added to all four regional Environment Divisions and to the central Environment Department. The Bank is now reviewing the results of that effort.

In late 1991 the Bank commissioned an Independent Review of the Sardar Sarovar (Narmada) dam and reservoir projects in western India. The report identified weaknesses in the Bank's appraisal of the projects, in the borrowers' implementation, and in the Bank's supervision. The review recommended improvements in how the Bank prepares and manages projects that involve resettlement (see box 5-2).

The Environment Department's Resettlement Research Program is carrying out a Bankwide review of resettlement to assess the effectiveness of Bank policy and the institution's ability to address resettlement in future work. The study will build on regional portfolio analyses and commissioned studies of special factors that constrain resettlement in international development projects in order to develop a broadly based strategy for improvement.

The Bank also encourages improvements in resettlement through its continuing international training and conference program. In May 1992 the Environment Department and the Environment Division of the Latin America and Caribbean Technical Department sponsored an international conference in Brazil on involuntary resettlement in Latin America. Preceding UNCED by three weeks, the conference was regionwide in scope, with participation by most Latin American countries, as well as by China and India. University researchers, activist organizations and grass-roots NGOs also took part. The conference focused on both policy formulation and operational methods, covering topics such as monitoring techniques, collective bargaining, social and environmental impact assessment, and development of national policy. This was the last of three international conferences organized by the Bank on resettlement; others took place in Asia in 1989 and in Africa in 1991.

The OED has launched a review of involuntary resettlement in Bank-supported energy and agricultural projects. Four case studies have been initiated: hydroelectric projects in Ghana and Thailand and two irrigation projects in India. The objective of the review is to ascertain, from the perspective of the settlers themselves, how resettlement was carried out, the impact of relocation on the affected people, and the degree to which their economic livelihood has been restored. The study, which will cover sociological, environmental, legal, and economic issues, is expected to be completed next year.

Box 5-2. Learning from Narmada

The Sardar Sarovar (Narmada) Dam and Power Project and Water Delivery and Drainage Project were approved by the Bank in March 1985 to bring water (for households, agriculture, and industry), electricity, and employment opportunities to one of the poorest and most drought-prone regions of western India. From the projects' inception in the 1980s, there was concern about the impact of resettlement. This concern grew in the late 1980s and focused, to a large extent, on the resettlement policies and programs actually being offered by the states involved—Gujarat, Maharashtra, and Madhya Pradesh. In early 1991 the president of the World Bank commissioned an independent review of the implementation of the resettlement and rehabilitation activities and the environmental aspects of the Sardar Sarovar projects.

The Independent Review report identified a number of deficiencies in the Bank's appraisal of the projects, in the borrower's implementation, and in the Bank's supervision. It found that performance under the projects has clearly fallen short of what is called for under Bank policies and guidelines and the policies of the government of India.

The problems highlighted by the Independent Review report call for a comprehensive and vigorous response. The Bank is currently discussing the elements of such a comprehensive response and will shortly be making its decision publicly known.

The experience with the Independent Review carries lessons that extend beyond the Narmada projects. Some of these—such as the critical importance of good baseline data and effective local consultation prior to appraisal—reinforce messages emerging from the Bank's own monitoring and evaluation work.

The review also points up the complexity of resettlement issues and the need for significant strengthening of both the Bank's and the borrower's capacity to address these issues in major projects. Supervision inputs in the Narmada projects have been about ten times the Bank's average, and yet deficiencies have persisted.

Indigenous Peoples and the Environment

The past decade has witnessed growing recognition of the practical role indigenous peoples can play in the conservation of fragile ecosystems such as rainforests, arid and semiarid rangelands, and upland watersheds. The world's remaining indigenous peoples—estimated to number more than 250 million in seventy countries—possess knowledge fundamental to the sustainable management of resources in these regions.

The Bank has continued to gain experience in designing projects so as to mitigate the adverse effects of development projects on the natural and cultural resources of indigenous peoples. In September 1991 the Operational Directive on Indigenous Peoples, which expands on a policy set in 1982, was issued. Drawing on experience accumulated over the past ten years, the operational directive provides guidelines for Bank-supported projects that affect indigenous people and states that Bank staff must ensure the "informed participation" of indigenous people in the preparation of development plans and in project design, implementation, and evaluation. With an understanding of local preferences, the Bank is better able to incorporate indigenous knowledge into project approaches. In cooperation with the Center for Indigenous Knowledge, the Environment Department prepared a Bank discussion paper entitled *Using Indigenous Knowledge in Agricultural Development* (Warren 1991). Region-specific technical papers are being prepared to support the implementation of the directive.

Much of the world's biodiversity lies within the traditional territories of indigenous peoples. Strategies for maintaining this biodiversity can only benefit by drawing on indigenous knowledge and understanding of the natural environment. "The Social Challenge of Biodiversity Conservation Projects" (World Bank 1992d) pulled together articles on innovative approaches to involving indigenous people in conservation activities. A background paper for *World Development Report 1992* on indigenous views of land and the environment (Davis 1991) looked at local approaches to natural resource management in three different indigenous societies. A biodiversity-mapping project now under way will use Geographic Information Systems to flag indigenous peoples' land issues early in the planning of projects that affect protected areas.

Land Tenure

In fiscal 1992 the Bank reviewed its experiences with land tenure and "regularization" issues in Latin America, paying special attention to projects that have affected the resource base of indigenous people. A summary paper, "Protecting Amerindian Lands: A Review of World Bank Experience with Indigenous Land Regularization Programs in Lowland South America" (Wali and Davis 1992), reviews the operational problems encountered in indigenous land tenure or "regularization" programs in Bank-funded projects in lowland areas of South America. The paper focuses on these areas because of the unintended consequences that Bank-financed road construction, land settlement, and resource extraction projects have had on indigenous people. The review is particularly important because the Bank's new operational directives

108

on Involuntary Resettlement and on Indigenous Peoples emphasize the significance of land tenure security for the development of indigenous communities and the protection of their natural resources. The paper concludes that future Bank land tenure programs affecting indigenous peoples should be accompanied by more detailed baseline studies, active participation by NGOs and indigenous communities, technical assistance, and the institutional strengthening of programs designed to build on indigenous knowledge, consistent with the objectives of the operational directive.

Cultural Property

A new Operational Directive on Cultural Property—a refinement of an earlier operational policy note—now being prepared will define Bank policy on the conservation of cultural property in Bank-supported projects. "Cultural property" refers to sites, structures, or remains with archaeological, historical, religious, cultural, or aesthetic value. It is Bank policy to protect and, where feasible, to enhance a country's cultural property through its policy dialogue, lending operations, and economic and sector work. The operational directive will be grounded in the recognition that maintaining a society's cultural values is important to the sustainability of its development, particularly where those values are reflected in cultural property of national or regional significance.

The International Conference on Culture and Development in Africa, which took place in April 1992, was the first large forum held at the Bank to address the links between culture, environment, and development. Sponsored by the governments of Norway and Sweden, the Ford Foundation, and the Bank, the conference discussed policies and actions needed to bring the cultural dimension into the mainstream of development planning in Sub-Saharan Africa.

Social Analysis in Bank Project and Sector Work

As the range of social and cultural factors involved in Bank policy, project, and sector work has expanded, a need has grown to address them through a unified set of guidelines on social analysis throughout the Bank. In fiscal 1992 the Bank initiated two broad sociological reviews to assess experience, best practices, and existing weaknesses in the use of social analysis in two important areas of Bank work: the preparation and design of Bank-financed projects, and Bank sector studies. Both will feed into the development of policy and operational guidelines; a Bank-wide working group has been formed to prepare an Operational Directive on Social Appraisal of Projects.

The first review—on social analysis in Bank project design and appraisal—focuses on five sectors: population and health, education, urban development, agriculture, and energy. The study compares the Bank's use of social analysis between fiscal 1979–81 and fiscal 1989–91. The preliminary results indicate that the Bank's project portfolio today is more sensitive than before to local social organizations, equity issues, and cultural concerns. More projects target the poor, disadvantaged, or underserved. Projects increasingly use social analysis to identify the main groups of social actors in a project area and to develop new ways of involving local populations in project activities.

The second review compares the Bank's sector work in 1981 and 1991 to examine the incorporation of social issues into the sectoral planning process and country dialogue. In comparison with the situation of a decade ago, significantly greater attention is now being given to such social issues as regional and gender equity, the distribution of project benefits, and poverty. Other important issues—for example, the role of governance and of various social actors in development policy and programs, popular participation in decisionmaking, the need to recognize local interests and capabilities, and long-term impacts—are gradually entering into the Bank's sectoral planning and reporting.

Environmental Information and Education

National Environmental Information Systems

In many countries, whether industrial or developing, environmental data are often incomplete or site-specific, making it difficult to extrapolate the results for the country as a whole. Yet estimates based on such data are routinely made. Although remote-sensing techniques are improving rapidly, providing scientists with more comprehensive pictures of environmental deterioration on regional and global scales, it is still difficult to get a good understanding of environmental degradation at local or project levels without carrying out extensive and expensive baseline studies on the ground.

In order to evolve realistic and sustainable management strategies, economists and planners must have detailed knowledge of the state of their country's natural resource base. Of particular importance in this regard is the collection and processing of information on land use patterns, including soil and hydrologic conditions, vegetation cover, climate, and the results of past and present human activities.

The generation of relevant information on natural resources is central to three of the Bank's environmental activities—environmental assessment, support for environmental action plans, and related country strategies. Environmental assessments must take stock of the country's natural resources and need good land use information if they are to be of real value. Similarly, implementation of environmental action plans requires improved information on land resources and better information management systems in order to identify the country's pressing environmental concerns, determine priorities, and build up institutional capacities to address them.

The Bank has systematically begun to promote the use of natural resource information in environmental assessment programs. A technical paper addresses the use and management of resource and environmental information at the project and country levels, the determination of resource information needs, and the selection of information management systems.

Other continuing Bank programs include the Africa region's initiative on environment information systems (EIS) in Sub-Saharan Africa. The EIS program helps African countries establish operational national environmental information systems in order to establish information priorities for better resource management. The environmental information program in Nigeria and the environmental information management system in Ghana reviewed the status of resource information and were instrumental in developing national integrated environmental information systems (see chapter 4).

International Economics and Environmental Indicators

During fiscal 1992 the Bank's International Economics Department cooperated closely with the World Development Report core team to devise a set of environmental indicators for use in World Development Report 1992 and to respond to emerging environmental policy priorities throughout the Bank. Drawing from extensive in-house and outside sources, a mainframe file of more than 400 time-series of primary environmental indicators was created, covering a wide range of topics and years. This data base was used to produce the Environmental Data Appendix to World Development Report 1992 and will provide a foundation for combining environmental and economic information in policy development and in the preparation of future country strategy papers, environmental action plans, and country economic papers.

Environmental information is being widely disseminated within and outside the Bank. An environmental appendix has been attached to the 1992 Social Indicators of Development, and a preliminary set of environmental indicators is available through the Bank's Economic and Social Database, as well as through the PC-driven Socio-economic Time-Series Access and Retrieval System (*STARS*). A new *STARS* prototype will

allow users to access detailed sources and citations of i̇
specific indicators, thus giving "pedigree" to the inforn
The Environment Department has set up a small team
of improving environmental indicators and, in collabo
Bank's International Economics Department, is consid
ment of a publication on environmental indicators, buiİ
initiated for *World Development Report 1992.*

With the use of COMETS (Coordinated Output Module for the Evaluation of Text and Statistics), a prototype text analysis system, Bank environmental documents can now be evaluated to discern critical
environmental problems in member countries. Based on a hierarchical
dictionary, COMETS promises to expedite the time-intensive process of
researching individual documents by focusing on a set of key words and
concepts.

Environmental Education

Environmental education and awareness are important components of
any viable strategy to improve environmental information and to con-
front issues such as deforestation, desertification, loss of biodiversity,
and air and water pollution. Increasingly, countries are recognizing the
need to tailor environmental education for all levels. Curricula in primary and secondary schools and in the nonformal sector help build
citizen awareness of environmental concerns and reinforce community
support for conservation and environmental protection measures. In
much of the developing world, however, environmental awareness remains a goal, not a reality.

Bank investment in the education sector can play an important role in
boosting developing country capacity through support for teacher training, better curricula, and the improvement of environmental research
and training institutions. With this in mind, the Bank has initiated a
review of the current status of environmental education in Africa and in
Central and Eastern Europe, similar to the 1991 review of Asia.

Global Environmental Issues

The 1980s witnessed the emergence of a new global environmental
agenda with far more complexity and uncertainty than national agendas. It does not lend itself to solutions based on a common legal framework (as in an individual country), regulatory controls, or the process of
national governance. Solutions to global environmental problems must
be based on collaboration among states, backed by negotiations and
binding agreements.

The Bank has responded to these new challenges by gearing up the Global Environment Facility (see chapter 3) and through its continuing work in funding projects aimed at preserving biodiversity, reducing the emission of greenhouse gases (particularly carbon dioxide), and curbing the production and use of ozone-depleting chemicals such as CFCs. The Climate Change and Biodiversity conventions signed in Rio de Janeiro are expected to serve as a basis for reducing global emissions of greenhouse gases and utilizing the world's remaining stock of wild plants and animals in a sustainable manner (see box 1-1).

Biodiversity

Destruction of forests, wetlands, and other ecosystems and the extinction of species are occurring at rates unprecedented in human history. Biological diversity is a matter of international concern. The Biodiversity Convention attempts to address two important questions: how can developing countries manage their resources in their own best interests? and how should the international community contribute to the protection of important biological resources? Bank work, both under the GEF and through the Bank's own lending and research activities, is intended to address these important global issues.

The concept of multiple-use reserves fits directly into the biodiversity conservation mandate of the GEF. By expanding and encouraging the sustainable use of products and services from rainforests, multiple-use reserves present an attractive alternative to more conventional conservation strategies. If people are allowed to live in and around protected areas and to benefit from them, they are more likely to manage resources sustainably. Well-designed and well-implemented multiple-use reserves can generate environmentally compatible forms of economic development. But better research and management techniques are still needed in setting up such reserves and in finding markets for their products.

The Bank has developed a set of guidelines for the design and management of multiple-use reserves. These guidelines address the social and legal aspects of these reserves, natural resource management, the economic and market viability of nontimber forest products, and the legal and social aspects of reserve management—such as land tenure, common property resources, cooperative mechanisms, the social aspects of marketing, and implications for indigenous peoples.

Global Warming

Scientists are now broadly agreed that atmospheric concentrations of the gases that could cause global warming—the greenhouse gases—are rising. But there is little consensus as to which areas would be worst affected or what the regional or global effects may be. The Climate Change Convention sets the stage for a concerted international effort to reduce greenhouse gases in order to lessen the risks of global climate change (see box 1-1).

Work continued in fiscal 1992 on methodologies that support the Bank's role in administering the GEF in relation to the issue of global warming. Research examined the costs of interventions in the energy sector and ways of calculating their effects. The uncertainties in current estimates of greenhouse gas emissions and their implications were also investigated, and work has been concluded on the implications of alternate principles for sharing the burden of reducing greenhouse gas emissions worldwide. The results of this research and a comprehensive framework for considering global warming issues were presented in May 1992 at a Bank seminar on global warming.

An analysis of carbon taxes, "Carbon Taxes, the Greenhouse Effect, and Developing Countries" (Shah and Larsen 1992) evaluates the case for carbon taxes in light of national interests, priorities in developing countries, and implications for global negotiations. The study argues that taxes based on the carbon content of fuel make economic sense for many large carbon-emitting countries for reasons of improved energy efficiency, equity, tax administration, and generation of funds for dealing with local environmental problems.

Related research (Larsen and Shah 1992b) offers a first approximation of the level of world energy subsidies and their implications for carbon dioxide emissions. Total world energy subsidies in 1990 are estimated to be more than $230 billion—equivalent in revenue terms to a negative global carbon tax of $40 per ton of carbon emitted. Elimination of subsidies would reduce carbon emissions in the subsidizing countries by about 21 percent. To achieve an equivalent reduction in OECD countries, a carbon tax of $50–$90 per ton would be needed, amounting to an annual cost of $14 billion.

A paper on tradable carbon emissions permits and international transfers (Larsen and Shah 1992a) argues that both tradable emission permits and emission taxes could ensure reductions in carbon emissions. But the allocation of tradable carbon emission permits based on GDP, or on population—the two most widely discussed schemes—are unlikely to receive broad international support, largely because each results in unacceptable costs to either high-income countries or poorer countries. Any viable treaty for reducing carbon emissions must equitably distribute the costs of compliance. The work on tradable permits is being extended to include Central and Eastern Europe and the former U.S.S.R.

114

Ozone Depletion

Bank policy research has supported the operational requirements of the
Interim Multilateral Fund under the Montreal Protocol on Substances
That Deplete the Ozone Layer. In work completed this fiscal year, the
Bank developed a methodology for calculating incremental costs—the
basis for reimbursements under the fund—and analyzed policies and
strategies that recipient countries can use to implement their obligations
under the protocol. The results of this research were subsequently applied in a case study of Egypt and disseminated to decisionmakers
through regional workshops sponsored by the UNEP in Asia, the Middle
East and North Africa, and Latin America and the Caribbean.

Current research is focused on operational interpretations of the incremental cost criterion and on determining the unit abatement costs of
phasing out ozone-depleting substances (such as CFCs) in a variety of
sectors. The latter effort will assist in ranking Bank-funded projects to
ensure that the overall program is cost-effective.

Management and Prevention of Disasters

Natural disasters cause significant loss of life and property every year.
During the 1980s roughly 500 million people were affected by earth-
quakes, typhoons, volcanic eruptions, tsunamis, floods, droughts, and
other disasters. Vulnerability to disasters is often compounded by environmental degradation and increases with the use of inappropriate or
obsolete technologies, lack of information and of access to mitigation
measures, and ill-prepared institutions.

A joint effort by the UNDP, the World Bank, and UNCHS-Habitat is
examining this combined problem of urban vulnerability and environmental degradation in three countries, Brazil, Philippines, and Turkey.
The study will outline strategies for disaster prevention, mitigation, and
recovery. A conference sponsored by the Bank also addressed the relationship between environmental degradation and disaster vulnerability
in cities, highlighting effective environmental-based strategies for risk
management and the implications for the Bank.

Operations Evaluation

As in previous years, the Bank's Operations Evaluation Department
(OED) addressed environmental issues in its review of project completion
reports and in its own performance audit work. Since 1988 the OED's
annual review has been thematic, and this year's review focuses on the
environment. The review discusses both "brown issues" that affect

urban areas—particularly air pollution, industrial wastes, and water supply and sanitation—and "green issues" such as forestry, land settlement, fisheries, irrigation, agriculture, and rural development.

Special OED sector studies focused this year on forestry, water supply, environment in Brazil, and renewable resource management in agriculture. (The water and agriculture reviews are described in the discussions of those sectors, above).

Annual Review of Evaluation Results

The OED's "Annual Review of Evaluation Results 1991" places specific emphasis on environmental performance in Bank-funded projects. Most of the projects evaluated were prepared prior to the Bank's reorganization in 1987 and were completed before the 1989 introduction of the Operational Directive on Environmental Assessment. Accordingly, many of the shortcomings identified by the OED are now systematically addressed in the environmental assessment process.

One of the OED's main conclusions is the need for *strengthened project supervision* and greater attention to environmental matters in the review of completed projects. The Bank's first review of the environmental assessment process similarly recommends that the strong environmental emphasis given to project preparation and appraisal must also be accorded project supervision.

A second finding of the OED review is a possible positive *linkage between strong environmental performance and strong project performance* in other areas—economic, financial, and institutional, for example. Greater consideration should be given to this hypothesis, especially in light of the Bank's new Operational Directive on Environmental Assessment and other strengthened environmental policies now in place.

The OED report focused on several other issues, such as the importance of *strengthening institutional capacity*, especially in the urban and agricultural sectors. This is particularly crucial given the growing number of stand-alone environmental and technical assistance projects, which are designed to reform the policy and institutional frameworks for national environmental decisionmaking.

Greater attention should be given to the *macroeconomic policy framework* that determines the use and management of natural resources. The OED report notes that the Bank's past track record in incorporating environmental concerns into country economic strategy and policy work has been inconsistent. With the new Operational Directive on Environmental Action Plans, however, the Bank's policy framework has been strengthened, and environmental priorities and the associated investment strategy should be clearer. It is important to ensure that improved environmental policies and strategies filter down to project design and implementation.

Finally, the review highlights the still limited understanding of the Bank and its borrowers about the complex *relations between poverty and environmental degradation*. This weakness is especially serious where the ecosystems on which poor people depend are threatened by overpopulation, deforestation, soil erosion, water scarcity, and other forms of environmental stress.

Evaluating Bank-Supported Projects in Brazil

During fiscal 1992 the OED completed a review of the Bank's environmental record in Brazil, based on four case studies of large-scale projects: industrial pollution control and urban environmental management in São Paulo; cross-sectoral water resource use and involuntary resettlement in the São Francisco River Valley; the impact of rail, road, and port construction in the Carajas mining region and its effects on Amerindian populations; and the effects of road and rural development projects on tropical forests and other environmental resources in the Northwest region of Amazonia, which includes the state of Rondônia and parts of Mato Grosso.

The *São Paulo* Industrial Pollution Control Project was initially designed to focus on the São Paulo Metropolitan Area but was later extended to include the entire state of São Paulo, covering 250,000 square kilometers, with a population of 30 million. Large-scale industrial pollution control projects approved in 1980 and 1987 were part of a broader program to provide basic sanitation and reduce air pollution in the region. The OED report found that these projects had a significant impact on levels of industrial pollution and hence on air and water quality, notably in Cubatão, where air pollution levels were reduced by more than half between 1984 and 1988. In metropolitan São Paulo, however, air pollution from vehicle emissions continues to be a serious problem. The report also recognized the need for better coordination of policies, programs, and investments for control of water pollution.

The *São Francisco River* flows for about 2,700 kilometers through five states. More than half of the river's 640,000-square-kilometer drainage basin is located in an area known as the "Drought Polygon," characterized by highly irregular rainfall patterns. Beginning in the 1970s, Brazil, with Bank assistance, began an ambitious but loosely coordinated large-scale development program for the middle and lower river basin in an attempt to regulate water flow better, increase power generation, boost agricultural production, and create jobs. Development centered on building hydroelectric dams and extensive public and private irrigation systems. The program was not without problems. Rural resettlement in connection with the Paulo Afonso IV Hydropower ("Sobradinho") Project was only partially successful. Although the Lower São Francisco Polders and Second Irrigation projects successfully met their primary objectives, they were, in effect, little more than emergency operations designed to compensate for the construction of the Sobradinho Dam, about 800 kilometers upstream. The subsequent Itaparica Resettlement and Irrigation Project transferred 40,000 people to new towns and rural villages in 1987–88, but costly irrigation facilities have not yet become fully operational.

The Carajas Project (1982) involved major investments—totaling about $4 billion—in transport, infrastructure, and mining facilities along a 900-kilometer corridor in eastern Amazonia, linking one of the world's richest mineral deposits to a coastal terminal. Since 1970 the area has experienced one of Amazonia's highest rates of deforestation, with associated environmental degradation. Although the project contained numerous environmental protection components—for the establishment of conservation tracts, greenbelt buffer zones, ecological stations, and biotic inventories—environmental controls and assessment procedures were found to be too limited in geographic coverage. More successful has been a special project to help protect about 130 local Amerindian communities, some of whose members have clearly benefited from land demarcation and the provision of health care. Remaining environmental threats include the increasing extraction of fuelwood for charcoal production and the expansion of swidden agriculture by subsistence farmers.

In May 1981 the Brazilian government formally launched a major investment program in the agricultural frontier areas of Rondônia and western Mato Grosso. *The Northwest Integrated Development Project* (POLONOROESTE) sought to manage the increasing flow of migrants from the south in a sustainable manner and to minimize the negative impacts on the environment by expanding infrastructure and supporting agriculture and social services.

A midterm review of the project in 1984 highlighted the differences between the assumptions under which the program was planned and those under which it was being implemented. The project was affected by unexpectedly high migration of settlers, leading to unchecked deforestation and continued encroachment into unsuitable areas of marginal soil fertility; inadequate and late disbursement of counterpart funds because of the difficult fiscal situation in Brazil; a shortage of the investment credit needed to establish perennial crops; and overcentralized project management and ineffective integration of participating agencies. Roads were built on time, but agricultural support services, community facilities, and environmental and Amerindian protection measures lagged behind. The borrower and the Bank agreed to an informal suspension of disbursements until measures could be taken to correct these problems. The suspension was in effect from March through August 1985.

Since 1985 the program has been substantially reoriented. State environmental protection agencies have been established in both Mato Grosso and Rondônia. A major effort was made to protect the Pantanal wetlands from further ecological damage. Tree crops were planted in a number of areas, and more funds were devoted to environmental monitoring and protection activities. By 1990 about 80 percent of the region's indigenous population was residing in legally demarcated reserves, totaling some 9.9 million hectares—a much higher proportion than at the start of the program.

The OED report found that the Bank approached these projects with a concern for the environment and made considerable efforts to broaden its traditional approach to project development. But in retrospect, many of the decisions made at preparation and appraisal took too little account of the social and physical environment. This was partly because the Bank lacked enough knowledge about the socioeconomic context into which it was lending, and partly because its expertise in environmental matters was still very limited. In the past fifteen years, with the growth of environmental awareness and expertise, environmental concerns have begun to be much better integrated into economic development initiatives. The experience reviewed offers important lessons relevant to current practice in Bank operations generally.

The report's recommendations for improved environmental protection call for strengthening of the borrower's environmental institutional and technical capacity, generation of greater public awareness and participation, and improvement of regulations and of economic incentives for sustainable resource use. Environmental assessment and management should be strengthened by means of thorough and broadly based initial project assessment and with special attention to the potential environmental consequences of macroeconomic and sectoral policies. Bank activities and procedures should continue to work toward improving the integration of environmental concerns into economic and sector work and the assessment of borrowers' lending commitment and capacity to achieve project environmental goals. In addition, the Bank should improve project supervision, monitoring, and evaluation. Finally, the OED report emphasizes the need for measures to guarantee protection of the natural environment and of vulnerable social groups—especially indigenous populations and people to be involuntarily resettled—after Bank financing has concluded.

Notes

1. Ernst Lutz, ed. Forthcoming. *Toward Improved Accounting for the Environment.* A World Bank Symposium. Washington, D.C.

2. Dean T. Jamison and W. Henry Mosley. Forthcoming. *Disease Control Priorities in Developing Countries.* 2 vols. New York: Oxford University Press.

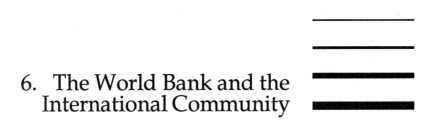

6. The World Bank and the International Community

Interagency Cooperation

The World Bank is continuing its efforts to cooperate on issues of environmentally sound development policies with other multilateral institutions, especially the UNEP and the UNDP. In particular, the implementation of the funding mechanism for both the Montreal Protocol and the GEF institutionalizes policy coordination between the Bank and these two agencies.

At the country level, the Bank has broadened its efforts to cooperate with the UNDP, the United Nations Children's Fund (UNICEF), and the International Fund for Agricultural Development (IFAD) in the preparation and follow-up of poverty and human development assessments. At the project level, regular institutional collaborators include the UNDP, UNICEF, the World Health Organization (WHO), the International Labour Organization (ILO), the Food and Agriculture Organization of the United Nations (FAO), and the World Food Programme. To strengthen its knowledge and research base, the Bank regularly coordinates work on policy analysis with other agencies of the United Nations system. Currently, the Bank and the UNDP are collaborating on a water and sanitation program designed to devise poverty alleviation strategies on the basis of community institutions and low-cost technologies. The Energy Sector Management Assistance Program (ESMAP) represents joint Bank-UNDP efforts in the energy sector. Together with the FAO and the UNDP, the Bank serves as a cosponsor of the Consultative Group on International Agricultural Research (CGIAR), an association of public and private sector donors supporting a network of international agricultural research centers.

In the follow-up to UNCED, the Bank is participating actively in the recently created Administrative Committee on Coordination (ACC) Task Force on Environment and Development. The task force will consider guidelines for an interagency division of labor in implementing Agenda

21, including arrangements to improve coordination and reporting to the Sustainable Development Commission by the United Nations system.

Regional Institutions

Cooperation with the European Community and the Commission of the European Communities has been stepped up during the past fiscal year, and a new position has been created in the Bank's European office to address liaison issues full time. The Bank actively pursues a dialogue with the OECD and its Development Assistance Committee (DAC) on environmental policies and practices of mutual concern to bilateral and multilateral aid donors. The Bank and DAC regularly exchange data on aid flows, debt, and financial transfers. Dialogue focuses on issues of governance, participatory development, tied aid, and technical cooperation.

The Bank's relationship with the various regional development banks—the African Development Bank (AfDB), the Asian Development Bank (ADB), the Inter-American Development Bank (IDB) and the European Bank for Reconstruction and Development (EBRD)—continues to be close. The Bank has been involved in numerous joint initiatives with all of these institutions; cofinancing arrangements cover both sector and project lending. Collaboration with the International Monetary Fund (IMF) is, of course, significant, but it has been particularly close in the context of the Central and Eastern European countries' transition to market economies. The Bank and the IMF are also cooperating in assisting new members from the former U.S.S.R.

External Training and the Economic Development Institute

During fiscal 1992 the World Bank's Economic Development Institute (EDI) carried out a number of environment-related activities, concentrating mainly on information dissemination and training for borrowing countries. Environment is one of the EDI's four cross-sectoral themes. Environmental training, provided at both the policy and project levels, is promoted and conducted through stand-alone activities or within sectoral training in collaboration with sectoral divisions, depending on the training needs of borrowing countries. These efforts were bolstered this year with the recruitment of three environmental specialists and the development of an environmental training strategy for the coming two years.

The EDI organized a meeting of senior decisionmakers from around the world as part of the preparations for *World Development Report 1992,* which was devoted to the theme "Development and the Environment." Recommendations from the meeting were incorporated into the report.

Together with the 1992 World Development Report team and the External Affairs Department, the EDI helped produce a television documentary based on the main messages of *World Development Report 1992.* The documentary, which was presented at the Earth Summit, showed how various environmental and development problems can be solved by raising incomes, improving technological capacities, and placing greater reliance on market forces. Four case studies illustrating linkages between development and the environment were highlighted: deforestation in Rondônia, Brazil; desertification in Burkina Faso; sanitation problems in Karachi, Pakistan; and industrial pollution in Katowice, Poland.

The EDI continued to work closely with countries belonging to the Amazonian Cooperation Treaty (ACT), hosting a meeting of senior policy staff to incorporate economic analysis into policy formulations designed for the Amazon. These discussions resulted in the drafting of a policy statement, "Amazonia Sin Mitos." The EDI also commissioned ACT to undertake the translation into Spanish of the Bank's *Environmental Assessment Sourcebook* for environmental training in Latin America and the Caribbean.

The EDI conducted seminars on natural resource development and environmental management in Sub-Saharan Africa and in the arid areas of the Middle East and North Africa. A seminar on forest management for sustainable development that was held in Malaysia for Southeast Asian and Pacific countries will be followed up by activities in each country designed to strengthen local institutions.

The EDI carried out environmental training sessions for development bankers, senior managers, and advisers in francophone Africa and in Latin America, concentrating on the environmental impacts of energy investments. Training sessions focusing on water resources and the environment were conducted in Africa, Asia, and Central Europe, and programs on urban services and environmental management in East Asia, Eastern Europe, and Latin America.

In collaboration with the Environment Division of the Latin America and Caribbean region's Technical Department, the EDI formulated a plan for in-country training in environmental assessment and is developing appropriate materials. It undertook activities in Chile and Colombia at the advanced technical and intermediate managerial levels, respectively.

The World Bank and the NGO Community

The Bank considers NGOs vital participants in the effort to achieve environmentally sustainable economic growth and encourages NGO involvement at the project level. In fiscal 1992, 66 (or about one-third) of the 222 projects approved by the Bank's Board of Executive Directors had NGO participation. Ten (15 percent) of the relevant projects were free-standing environmental operations—in Bangladesh, Brazil (two projects), Haiti, India (two projects), Kenya, Mali, Pakistan, and Tanzania. Of the NGOs involved, 76 percent were either indigenous intermediary NGOs or grass-roots groups based in borrowing countries.

Consultation with NGOs from the earliest stages of project design can be essential to operational and policymaking success. The Bank's *Monthly Operational Summary*, which categorizes potential projects according to nature, magnitude, and sensitivity to environmental issues, is mailed to nearly 400 NGOs worldwide to facilitate close interaction. In addition, the *Environmental Bulletin*, published quarterly, enables the Bank's Environment Department to apprise a readership of 15,000 NGOs, UN agencies, governments, academics, and concerned individuals of environment-related Bank projects, current events, conferences, seminars, workshops, training programs, and publications. A range of operational directives explicitly addresses questions of NGO involvement. In particular, the Operational Directive on Environmental Assessment provides guidance on the disclosure of information to local groups and NGOs.

NGOs are increasingly participating in Bank policy discussions on environmental matters. Following last year's successful NGO consultation on the draft of the Bank's forest sector policy paper, the Bank organized two consultations in May 1992 to facilitate NGO input into reviews of Bank policy on energy conservation and on management of water resources. In addition, NGOs made significant contributions to *World Development Report 1992*.

The Global Environment Facility also draws on expertise from nongovernmental organizations. NGO consultations were organized prior to the semiannual GEF Participants' Meetings held in December 1991 and in April–May 1992. Parallel meetings of this kind will henceforth be held regularly. NGOs may submit a proposal for regular GEF funding so long as that proposal has been approved by the government of the country in which the project will be carried out. In addition, a $5.0 million grant "window" for NGOs, administered by the UNDP, has been set up to support NGO initiatives in biodiversity.

The NGO–World Bank Committee is the principal vehicle for policy dialogue between the Bank and the NGO community. Formed in 1982, the committee provides an opportunity for exploration of policy issues by twenty-six NGO leaders from around the world and by Bank senior managers. In October 1991 the committee held its eleventh annual meeting, in Suraj Kund, India. Three broad themes are currently under consideration: structural adjustment and poverty, funding mechanisms for NGOs, and participatory development.

The dialogue in the NGO–World Bank Committee over the past couple of years was a catalyst for the initiation in fiscal 1992 of a three-year Bankwide program on participatory development. With the help of a $1.3 million trust fund established by the Swedish International Development Authority, this learning exercise is seeking to develop and document participatory Bank operational activities (many of which involve NGOs); accelerate Bank learning from various other efforts related to participation taking place both inside the Bank and elsewhere; and investigate any modifications that the Bank may need to make in its operational practices to encourage wider participation.

Annex A. Organizational Responsibilities for Environmental Activities

The World Bank's formal structure for carrying out environment-related activities consists of a central Environment Department, regional Environment Divisions, and a growing number of environmental units within country departments. The Bank's Legal Department has its own environment unit, and the Economic Development Institute has environment as a major cross-sectional theme in its training activities for borrowing countries. In addition, senior specialists with environmental expertise are increasingly being integrated into operational units, adding further environmental capacity to the Bank's activities.

The central Environment Department, located in the Vice Presidency for Sector and Operations Policy (OSP), is a policy-oriented, interdisciplinary group that is responsible for planning, formulating, and coordinating the Bank's overall environmental policies and approaches. It recommends environmental and social policies, initiatives, guidelines, and standards to Bank management.

The Environment Department works closely with regional operations departments, particularly with the regional Environment Divisions, in the implementation of Bank policy and consults with the Legal Department. It provides policy interpretation and strategic guidance, assists in the preparation and analysis of country and sector environmental strategies and action plans, and identifies best practices and practical means of project implementation. The department also works with the regional Technical Departments to ensure that the social and environmental impact assessment process is effectively integrated into the Bank's decisionmaking and to support the development of effective environmental institutions in borrowing countries.

The Environment Department's emphasis is on the integration of environmental concerns into the Bank's activities through cross-sectoral and cross-regional policies, with the aim of ensuring consistent application of policy directives and guidelines in the different geographic regions. It also helps in transferring experience gained from one region to another, initiates the development of standards and guidelines, and is responsible for monitoring the environmental assessment process and preparing the Bank's annual review of environmental assessment.

The Environment Department houses the Office of the Administrator of the Global Environment Facility (GEF), which plays a central role in coordinating the activities of the three GEF implementing agencies (the UNDP, the UNEP, and the World Bank). The administrator's office organizes the biannual Participants' Meetings and implements the GEF communications strategy. The GEF Office of the Operations Coordinator, also located in the Environment Department, coordinates projects funded by the GEF and the Bank with the regional operations departments and provides procedural guidelines and assistance for developing, processing, and supervising all GEF projects. The Office of the Coordinator serves as the center for communications between the Bank and outside parties.

The Environment Divisions in the four regional Technical Departments work closely with the country departments. They have a review and clearance responsibility for environmental assessments and review functions for environmental action plans. They also provide project support in specialized areas when such support is required by the country departments.

Country departments are at various stages in integrating environmental concerns into their routine operations. Some departments have incorporated environment units into their organizational structure and are defining a strategic direction for environmental work in their respective countries. Others rely more heavily on the regional Environment Divisions for assistance and guidance. Four country departments, covering twenty-five countries, now have units dedicated to environmental issues. Consultants are often hired to carry out specific environmental tasks.

Collaboration between the Environment Department and the External Affairs Department is growing and will continue. Areas for cooperation include following up on UNCED, monitoring environmental concerns of Bank policy interest in major international forums, and strengthening coordination on environmental and development issues within the United Nations system.

The Legal Department, through its Environmental Affairs Unit, has continued to provide advice on the legal and institutional framework for environment and natural resource management both in sector work and in specific operations. It provides advice on all legal issues arising under the GEF and other environment-related programs, such as the Mediterranean Environmental Technical Assistance Programme (METAP) and the Pilot Program for the Brazilian Rainforest.

The Operations Evaluation Department (OED) plays an important role in the environmental agenda of the Bank. Although the OED does not have an environmental division as such, selected projects are evaluated for their environmental impacts in various sectors within the OED, and the department has undertaken several specific environmental case studies. The Economic Development Institute (EDI) and the International Finance Corporation (IFC) each have an environmental program and responsibilities. The IFC's activities will be described this year in a separate report, *The IFC and the Environment: 1992 Annual Review*. The Development Economics Vice Presidency is also active in environment-related work.

The number of staff and of staff-years devoted to environmental work are difficult to measure accurately because of the extent to which these services are embedded in routine operations and the growing integration of environmental experts into operations. It is estimated, however, that 140 higher-level staff and 51 support staff are engaged in full-time environmental activities in the Environment Department and in the four regional Environment Divisions. On the basis of time recorded by these staff members, other staff, and long-term consultants, about 279 staff-years were devoted to environment and forestry activities in fiscal 1992.

Annex B. Illustrative List of Projects with Environmental Components Approved in Fiscal 1992

This annex provides details on projects approved in fiscal 1992 that have environmental objectives or components. The list illustrates the wide range of environmental concerns addressed by Bank projects and includes both free-standing environmental projects (project titles in italics) and projects with significant environmental components. Projects are deemed "primarily" environmental, or "free-standing," if either the costs of environmental protection measures or the environmental benefits accruing from the project exceed 50 percent of total project costs or benefits. They are considered to have a "significant environmental component" if the environmental protection costs or environmental benefits are in excess of 10 percent of total project costs or benefits.

Country	Project	Environmental component
Africa		
Angola	*Lobito-Benguela Urban Environmental Rehabilitation Project*	Provide clean urban water supply and environmental sanitation through rehabilitation and expansion of the water distribution and sanitary sewer systems; rehabilitate solid waste management systems and storm drainage and erosion control networks; conduct programs in sanitary and environmental education and urban revegetation; provide technical assistance and training in defining policy issues and action plans for environmental management; conduct studies to reorganize institutions and set economic water and sewer tariffs, define policy issues and action plans for environmental management and monitoring, and develop a Geographic Information System and land registration pilot program

Country	Project	Environmental component
Benin	Urban Rehabilitation and Management Project	Support rehabilitation of infrastructure and improve community-based environmental sanitation in the two largest cities
	Natural Resources Management Project	Support pilot operations for land, natural forest resource, and land-tenure management, leading to mapping and recording of individual and community rights in a public registry and the elaboration of land tenure legislation; conduct adaptive research programs and experiments involving soil and water management and other activities; provide training and education for farmers and support staff; support poaching controls in the national parks and reinforcement of forestry posts; conduct studies toward the elaboration of a natural resources management master plan and on the possibility of creating and managing a national fund for natural resources to ensure sustainability after the project; strengthen local capacity for planning and monitoring natural resource management
Burundi	Water Supply Sector Project	Construct rural water supply systems in nine provinces; develop and protect about 3,000 springs; assist with capacity building in the Department of Rural Water Resources by providing expertise, equipment, and training
Equatorial Guinea	Second Petroleum Technical Assistance Project	Provide technical assistance for monitoring and developing gas fields to ensure maximum rate of recovery; prevent energy waste and pollution caused by gas flaring
Ghana	National Feeder Roads Rehabilitation and Maintenance Project	Support program to plant fruit trees alongside feeder roads to prevent soil erosion

Country	Project	Environmental component
Ghana (continued)	National Agricultural Extension Project	Assist in achieving sustained agricultural production by streamlining and strengthening agricultural extension systems; support human resource development by providing teaching materials and farm and laboratory equipment and by upgrading teaching staff of agricultural colleges
Kenya	*Protected Areas and Wildlife Services Project*	Develop institutional capacity of Kenya Wildlife Service through technical assistance and training; rehabilitate and maintain park reserve infrastructure; establish and operate community wildlife program and wildlife enterprise development program; strengthen research and planning capacity (includes tourism studies and preparation of a Wetlands Master Plan); expand wildlife education program by building education centers and developing teaching materials and conservation-based curricula for schools; continue support for the elephant and rhinoceros special conservation programs; maintain an effective Wildlife Protection Unit to control poaching and ensure tourist security
Lesotho	Lesotho Highlands Water Project	Provide environmental protection measures and technical assistance to mitigate impacts of plan to export water from Lesotho to the industrial heartland of South Africa
	Infrastructure Engineering Project	Provide professional assistance for developing investment criteria and maintenance plans to facilitate development of the water authority; conduct loss-of-revenue analysis of lost water; take measures to rehabilitate water supply system; prepare long-range plan for sanitation
Mali	*Natural Resource Management Project*	Assist government and villagers in designing and implementing community natural resource management plans in about 150 villages; develop a park management plan; provide central government services with basic environmental monitoring facilities; conduct training and public awareness program on natural resource management; provide technical assistance, consultant services, applied research, and studies required for project implementation

Country	Project	Environmental component
Mauritius	Sugar Energy Development Project	Develop technology for efficient use of biomass for energy production; establish a bagasse-and-coal-fired power plant to displace existing diesel generator; provide technical assistance and training for program implementation and environmental monitoring
Niger	Agricultural Services Project	Strengthen agricultural, livestock, and environmental extension services; strengthen the linkages between agricultural extension and research
Nigeria	National Fadama Development Project	Construct shallow tubewells to increase irrigation potential; conduct aquifer studies and upgrade irrigation technologies; organize farmers for irrigation management; complete a full environmental assessment of future development of flood plains
	Environmental Management Project	Provide institutional strengthening to design, implement, monitor, and enforce environmental incentive systems and regulations; establish data collection system and information network to monitor environmental trends; finance the identification of specific investment projects critical for alleviating environmental degradation, as well as feasibility studies for projects to be carried out by government agencies; provide technical assistance and training for the institutional strengthening and studies components and laboratory equipment for an environmental information network
São Tomé and Principe	Agricultural Privatization and Smallholder Development Project	Assist in developing methods of diversified and sustainable growth in agriculture; support environmental protection measures through reform in the agricultural sector administration and support services

Country	Project	Environmental component
Tanzania	*Forest Resources Management Project*	Support revision of forest policy and implementation of required changes in legislation; advise on adjusting user fees to reflect the economic value of forest resources and on improving the system of royalty collection; carry out studies and related activities to assist the government in formulating a strategy for land tenure and land use planning policies; support training in social forestry and a pilot woodland management program

Asia

Bangladesh	*Forest Resources Management*	Establish forest management system responsive to economic, social, and environmental goals; prepare and implement forest management plans for established plantations and natural forests; improve forest resource information management system; integrate environmental and social factors into resource management; increase public participation in forest development; formulate plans for conservation areas; provide support for foresters' education and training and for mangrove research
China	Tarim Basin Irrigation Project	Rehabilitate and upgrade irrigation and drainage facilities by reclaiming areas of desert wasteland; finance an ecosystem restoration component designed to recover some of the natural forest and so prevent expansion of the desert
	Zouxian Thermal Power Project	Provide technical assistance for institution building in environmental planning, for studying the impact on air quality of thermal power expansion programs, and for developing methodologies for site selection that minimize adverse environmental impacts

Country	Project	Environmental component
China (continued)	Ship Waste Disposal Project	Reduce pollution of international and Chinese territorial waters through improved interport system for monitoring ships' wastes; prepare an oil spill abatement contingency plan; provide technical assistance to upgrade ships' waste and environmental monitoring capabilities for ports and coastal and international waters; initiate a marine ecosystem monitoring system (SEATRACK)
	Beijing Environmental Project	Construct sewer networks to prevent groundwater pollution; construct pressurized hot water piping to alleviate air pollution from burning coal; renovate and in some cases relocate several highly polluting industries; construct a sanitary landfill and procure equipment for municipal solid waste management; provide technical assistance for study of optimal natural resource management methods; provide training for key staff of the Environmental Protection Bureau in advanced environmental management methods
	Tianjin Urban Development and Environment Project	Increase efficiency and responsiveness of Tianjin's environmental management systems by providing technical assistance and training for solid waste management; support physical works to improve drainage, sewerage, and solid waste management; provide credit for investment in pollution control and waste minimization measures
India	Shrimp and Fish Culture Project	Provide environmental management and training and finance an environmental monitoring program to preserve ecologically fragile marine areas as part of the development of the brackish-water shrimp industry

Country	Project	Environmental component
India (continued)	*Maharashtra Forestry Project*	Reorganize public forest administration; improve state's technical capacity for forest regeneration and monitoring; increase local participation in development of forest sector; rationalize forest sector policies and regulations; support activities related to land treatment, including rehabilitation of wasteland and degraded lands, soil and water conservation, improvement of wildlife habitat, biodiversity conservation, village ecodevelopment, and farm forestry
	West Bengal Forestry Project	Regenerate or afforest degraded forestlands and mangrove areas; expand farm forestry; improve forestry research and plant propagation; survey and demarcate forestlands; train forestry staff; improve management of wildlife and protected areas
Indonesia	*BAPEDAL Development Technical Assistance Project*	Support five-year Environmental Impact Management Agency Development Plan by strengthening institutional capacity for environmental management and pollution control and designing and implementing pollution control systems and procedures; finance technical assistance for review of existing laws, regulations, and procedures relating to pollution control; assist in planning, establishing, and strengthening pollution control agencies and laboratories; provide technical assistance for development of a training program and prepare proposals for donor financing
	Second Irrigation Subsector Project	Provide technical assistance to strengthen institutional capacity for efficient management of water resources; institute monitoring systems and improve environmental assessment capabilities of water users' associations
	Third Kabupaten Roads Project	Strengthen nationwide systems and procedures for environmental analysis of road works; support studies assessing long-term, indirect environmental impact of road rehabilitation and improvement

Country	Project	Environmental component
Korea, Rep. of	Gas System Expansion Project	Strengthen infrastructure required for import and utilization of natural gas to improve energy efficiency and reduce emissions of sulfur dioxide
	Pusan and Taejon Sewerage Project	Support National Wastewater Treatment Plan to improve water quality in rivers by constructing sewage treatment plants in Pusan and Taejon regions; provide technical assistance to update the cities' Sewerage Master Plans; design a program to convert combined-type sewers to a hygienically superior separate system
Malaysia	Power System Development Project	Provide technical assistance to improve environmental monitoring and evaluation capabilities
Maldives	Third Fisheries Project	Provide technical assistance to the Ministry of Planning and Environment for monitoring key environmental parameters during construction of a port and a land-based cold-storage facility for fish
Nepal	Power Sector Efficiency Project	Provide technical assistance in identifying energy conservation measures, implementing a catchment management pilot plan to improve soil conservation and sediment control, and improving effectiveness of overall operating system
Pakistan	*Environmental Protection and Resource Conservation Project*	Strengthen federal and provincial environmental protection agencies; develop a framework for introducing environmental policy considerations into public and private investment decisions; develop environmental planning and management training; undertake activities to rehabilitate natural resources (watersheds, rangelands, wildlife populations), emphasizing community involvement, monitoring, and evaluation; finance technical assistance

136

Country	Project	Environmental component
Pakistan (continued)	Fordwah Eastern Sadiqia (South) Irrigation and Drainage Project	Control waterlogging and salinity and raise agricultural production through improved water management; increase delivery efficiency of canals and watercourses by installing canal lining, interceptor drains, and surface drains; monitor impact on groundwater table; support research on irrigation and drainage
	Domestic Energy Resources Development Project	Implement measures to mitigate potential environmental impact from development of oil and natural gas fields
Papua New Guinea	Oro Smallholder Oil Palm Development Project	Protect the habitat of the world's largest butterfly, an endangered species, as part of project to increase oil palm production and exports
Philippines	Engineering and Science Project	Bolster environmental studies programs in coordination with the development and strengthening of postgraduate programs in science and engineering education
Thailand	Third Power System Development Project	Assist the Electricity Generating Authority in optimizing its investment decisions; strengthen the environmental regulatory agencies in the power and mining sectors; support installation of an environmental monitoring network; finance technical assistance, training, and procurement of environmental monitoring equipment
	Fourth Highway Sector Project	Finance measures to improve road traffic safety, efficiency, and capacity, reduce vehicular air and noise pollution, and improve efficiency of road transport industry

Europe and Central Asia; Middle East and North Africa

Algeria	Sahara Regional Development Project	Support institutional development through establishment of a monitoring system for water resource use and water and soil quality and creation of an agency to operate and maintain drainage infrastructure; support studies, technical assistance, and training in the preparation of environmental assessments for future investments

Country	Project	Environmental component
Cyprus	Southeast Coast Sewerage and Drainage Project	Construct central sewage collection, treatment, and disposal system that includes the distribution of treated effluent for reuse and upgrading of existing stormwater drainage systems; provide technical assistance and training for the sewerage boards
Czech and Slovak Republic	Power and Environmental Improvement Project	Install equipment and improve operational efficiency to reduce pollution-causing lignite consumption; install flue gas desulfurization equipment to reduce emissions of sulfur dioxide; improve equipment for dust collection to reduce dust and flyash pollution; provide consulting services and staff training
Iran	Sistan River Flood Works Rehabilitation Project	Rehabilitate and upgrade existing flood control works and monitoring systems; strengthen institutional capacity to maintain the flood protection works; provide programs for early flood warning and emergency response and for resource management to address environmental, cultural property, and social concerns in the project area
Tunisia	Municipal Sector Investment Project	Strengthen municipal infrastructure for management of solid and liquid waste collection and disposal by upgrading and repairing existing systems and providing technical training
Yemen, Republic of	Land and Water Conservation Project	Provide improved groundwater irrigation conveyance systems and equipment for maintenance; provide equipment to demonstrate improved irrigation application technologies; provide equipment to strengthen the water monitoring system and for sand dune fixation, flood control, watershed management, and terrace stabilization; support training and technical assistance for the water resources and forest sectors

Latin America and the Caribbean

Country	Project	Environmental component
Argentina	Hydrocarbon Sector Engineering Project	Provide technical assistance to strengthen the government's hydrocarbon policymaking and regulatory capabilities; assist government efforts to develop and enforce environmental and safety standards

Country	Project	Environmental component
Brazil	*Rondônia Natural Resource Management Project*	Institute changes in policy, regulation, and investment programs to provide an incentive framework for sustainable development of Rondônia; conserve biodiversity while creating a basis for sustainable use of renewable resources; protect and enforce borders of conservation units and Amerindian reserves; control and prevent illegal deforestation; develop integrated farming systems and systems for sustainable forest agriculture and agroforestry; support services to implement agroecological zoning
	São Paulo Metropolitan Transport Decentralization Project	Support development of financial, institutional, and organizational policy for integrated multimodal transport; reduce air and noise pollution, fossil fuel consumption, and traffic congestion; improve access to employment, thus facilitating poverty reduction
	Water Sector Modernization Project	Finance formulation of a new regulatory framework for the water and wastes sector, including a detailed plan for institutional reform, drafts of proposed legislation and regulations, and definition of federal and state functions; prepare facilities for a proposed Water Demand Management and Systems Rehabilitation Project; expand and upgrade water supply and sewerage services
	National Industrial Pollution Control Project	Finance investments in pollution control to improve public health and living conditions of the population concentrated in and around industrialized areas; support participating states in establishing an integrated approach to solving pollution problems in a cost-effective manner; familiarize banking system with financing free-standing pollution control investments; strengthen institutional capabilities

Country	Project	Environmental component
Brazil *(continued)*	*Mato Grosso Natural Resource Management Project*	Assist the government to develop an incentives framework for sustainable development and conservation of biodiversity; support agroecological zoning, agroforestry, and regularization of land tenure in areas suitable for permanent agriculture; strengthen state institutions for the protection and management of forests and indigenous reserves and for agricultural services; support priority environmental management and monitoring activities
Chile	Transport Infrastructure Project	Increase efficiency of port activities and improve and monitor environmental conditions at project ports; prepare plans to prevent and control environmental damage from spills; improve management and disposal of ships' waste; establish an environmental monitoring and evaluation program to support future decisions on port activities
Colombia	Third National Roads Sector Project	Establish an environmental unit in the Ministry of Public Works and Transportation to prepare environmental guidelines and supervise impact assessment studies; improve road maintenance planning and environmental management practices; provide technical assistance, studies, and training in environmental control
Costa Rica	Agricultural Sector Investment and Institutional Development Project	Support sustainable agricultural growth by improving the efficiency and effectiveness of public sector institutions and their expenditures; increase public expenditure for agricultural research and extension services, land titling, and consolidation of settlements; develop an analytical framework to guide soil and crop management policies; assist in improving land use classification, assessing ecosystems susceptible to soil losses, and measuring the extent and cost of the actual or potential damage to the natural resource base; implement a program to demarcate the boundaries of national parks, biological reserves, and other protected areas

Country	Project	Environmental component
Haiti	*Forestry and Environmental Protection Project*	Provide technical and financial support for strengthening institutions in natural resource management and protection; provide training in forestry and agroforestry; finance programs to promote tree planting and soil conservation, expand research, and establish and manage national parks and biosphere reserves; improve management of forest reserves; support monitoring of land use; promote fuel-efficient charcoal stoves in urban areas
Honduras	Energy Sector Adjustment Program	Establish a comprehensive energy policy and regulatory framework; improve the efficiency of the national power company by progressively reducing electricity losses; provide technical assistance for an interfuel substitution study to address, among other things, concerns about deforestation through excessive use of fuelwood
Mexico	Irrigation and Drainage Sector Project	Assist government investment program to improve irrigation and drainage systems; strengthen institutional capacity of the National Water Commission; optimize use of land and water resources in the Irrigation District; monitor and prevent environmental and natural resource degradation; rehabilitate waterlogged or saline irrigated land
	Environmental Project	Support the government's efforts to carry out key environmental and natural resource protection functions; finance monitoring and control of water and air pollution, minimization of negative environmental impacts of investment projects, and conservation of biodiversity; strengthen institutions for sector management through a pilot decentralization program in as many as five states; strengthen regulatory frameworks by creating additional technical standards for pollution control and natural resource protection

Country	Project	Environmental component
Paraguay	Land Use Rationalization Project	Improve the information base to increase governmental effectiveness; strengthen institutions reponsible for land settlements and management and protection of natural resources; create a complete multipurpose rural land survey and a socioeconomic data base, including a geodetic grid; establish a Geographic Information System for economic classification of land use; create a program of studies to analyze institutional aspects of the agriculture sector, existing land-titling systems, policies affecting land use practices, environmental legislation and regulations, and the role of indigenous people in natural resource management
Trinidad and Tobago	Business Expansion and Industrial Restructuring Project	Promote development or restructuring of private export-oriented manufacturing or service firms; provide technical assistance to develop internationally accepted industrial standards, quality management, metrology, testing services, and improved environmental pollution control standards for evaluating investment proposals; strengthen the municipal planning division's capacity to review environmental impact assessments

Appendix C.   GEF Investment Projects Approved in Fiscal 1992

Country	Project	Description
Africa		
Mauritius	Sugar Bio-Energy Technology Project	Support first two-to-three-year phase of an investment program to improve energy efficiency and energy production in sugar mills; develop or locally adapt technologies for sugar biomass energy production, handling, and storage; train technical staff of bagasse-and-coal plants; support management and coordination of the Bagasse Energy Development Program, including environmental monitoring
Asia		
Bhutan	Trust Fund for Environmental Conservation	Support an integrated countrywide approach for forest conservation and preservation of biodiversity; test the feasibility of trust funds as a mechanism for supporting conservation of biodiversity; establish a Nature Conservation Division in Bhutan's Department of Forestry; establish national system of protected areas, prioritizing areas for protection and management; support management of two existing protected areas and development of one new protected area; provide funding for training foresters, ecologists, and natural resource managers and for inventories, research, and development of infrastructure

Country	Project	Description
China	Marine Environment Pollution Project	Assist the government of China in rehabilitating, modernizing, or expanding facilities at six ports for handling and disposing of ships' wastes; establish baseline conditions on international traffic, waste volumes, and handling and disposal arrangements; specify and design needed collection, monitoring, and disposal facilities; review and propose strengthening of institutional arrangements and environmental regulations; introduce new fees and fines to provide incentives for port-based disposal of ship-generated wastes; prepare a contingency plan for marine accidents and oil spills at each port

Europe and Central Asia; Middle East and North Africa

Poland	Forest Biodiversity Protection Project	Provide institutional support to the Ministry of Environment, Natural Resources, and Forestry to carry out biodiversity conservation management activities and protect biodiversity in two forests; finance pilot investments in air and soil monitoring equipment, a forest genebank, and a program to support the transition to ecological forestry in Poland

Latin America and the Caribbean

Ecuador	ENDESA/BOTROSA Afforestation Project (joint GEF-IFC project)	Finance the reforestation of 5,000 hectares of degraded former forestland; monitor prior conditions, timber growth, selective species growth rates, and ecological aspects of the replanted forest and the interaction of the replanted areas with remnant areas of tropical moist forest; evaluate social aspects and land use dynamics of the land purchasing program; monitor the employment, resource transfer, and multiplier effects generated by the project
Mexico	Biodiversity Conservation	Enhance the conservation of Mexico's biodiversity by supporting the management of eighteen protected areas selected for their contribution to protection of globally important biodiversity; support basic infrastructural development

Bibliography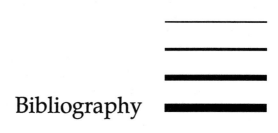

Publications

Titles published by the World Bank during fiscal 1992 may be obtained from the bookstores at the Bank offices in Washington, D.C., and Paris or through the Bank's authorized commercial distributors and depository libraries throughout the world.

Ahmed, Masood, and Gary P. Kutcher. 1992. *Irrigation Planning with Environmental Considerations: A Case Study of Pakistan's Indus Basin*. World Bank Technical Paper 166. Washington, D.C.

Bennett, Lynn. 1992. *Women, Poverty, and Productivity in India*. EDI Seminar Paper 43. Washington, D.C.: World Bank.

Birdsall, Nancy, and David Wheeler. 1992. "Trade Policy and Industrial Pollution in Latin America: Where Are the Pollution Havens?" In Patrick Low, ed., *International Trade and the Environment*. World Bank Discussion Paper 159. Washington, D.C.

Blackwell, Jonathan M., Roger N. Goodwillie, and Richard Webb. 1991. *Environment and Development in Africa: Selected Case Studies*. EDI Analytical Case Study 6. Washington, D.C.: World Bank.

Cernea, Michael M., ed. 1991. *Putting People First: Sociological Variables in Rural Development*. 2d ed., revised and expanded. New York: Oxford University Press.

Dejene, Alemneh, and José Olivares. 1991. *Integrating Environmental Issues into a Strategy for Sustainable Agricultural Development: The Case of Mozambique*. World Bank Technical Paper 146. Washington, D.C.

Feachem, Richard G. A., Tord Kjellstrom, Christopher J. L. Murray, Mead Over, and Margaret A. Phillips. 1992. *The Health of Adults in the Developing World*. New York: Oxford University Press.

Feder, Gershon, and David Feeny. 1991. "Land Tenure and Property Rights: Theory and Implications for Development Policy." *World Bank Economic Review* 5(1):135–53.

Herz, Barbara, Kalanidhi Subbarao, and Laura Raney. 1991. *Letting Girls Learn: Promising Approaches in Primary and Secondary Education*. World Bank Discussion Paper 133. Washington, D.C.

Hyde, William F., and David H. Newman, with Roger A. Sedjo. 1991. *Forest Economics and Policy Analysis: An Overview.* World Bank Discussion Paper 134. Washington, D.C.

Jodha, N. S. 1992. *Common Property Resources: A Missing Dimension of Development Strategies.* World Bank Discussion Paper 169. Washington, D.C.

Kreimer, Alcira, and Mohan Munasinghe, eds. 1992. *Environmental Management and Urban Vulnerability.* World Bank Discussion Paper 168. Washington D.C.

Le Moigne, Guy, Shawki Barghouti, Gershon Feder, Lisa Garbus, and Xie Mei, eds. 1992. *Country Experience with Water Resources Management: Economic, Institutional, Technological and Environmental Issues.* World Bank Technical Paper 175. Washington, D.C.

Lopez, Ramon, and Mario Niklitschek. 1991. "Dual Economic Growth in Poor Tropical Areas." *Journal of Development Economics* 36:189–211.

Low, Patrick, ed. 1992. *International Trade and the Environment.* World Bank Discussion Paper 159. Washington, D.C.

Lucas, Robert E. B., David Wheeler, and Hememala Hettige. 1992. "Economic Development, Environmental Regulation and the International Migration of Toxic Industrial Pollution: 1960–1988." In Patrick Low, *International Trade and the Environment.* World Bank Discussion Paper 159. Washington, D.C.

Markandya, Anil, and David W. Pearce. 1991. "Development, the Environment and the Social Rate of Discount." *World Bank Research Observer* 6(2):137–52.

Migot-Adholla, Shem, Peter Hazell, Benoît Blarel, and Frank Place. 1991. "Indigenous Land Rights Systems in Sub-Saharan Africa: A Constraint on Productivity?" *World Bank Economic Review* 5(1):155–75.

Preston, Lewis T. 1992. *Reducing Poverty and Protecting the Environment: A Call to Action* (address to the United Nations Conference on Environment and Development, June 1992). Washington, D.C.: The World Bank.

Warren, D. Michael. 1991. *Using Indigenous Knowledge in Agricultural Development.* World Bank Discussion Paper 127. Washington, D.C.

Wells, Michael, and Katrina Brandon, with Lee Hannah. 1992. *People and Parks: Linking Protected Area Management with Local Communities.* Washington, D.C.: World Bank, World Wildlife Fund, and U.S. Agency for International Development.

Wheeler, David, and Paul Martin. 1992. "Prices, Policies and the International Diffusion of Clean Technology: The Case of Wood Pulp Production." In Patrick Low, ed., *International Trade and the Environment.* World Bank Discussion Paper 159. Washington, D.C.

World Bank. 1991a. *Environmental Assessment Sourcebook.* Vol. 1. *Policies, Procedures, and Cross-Sectoral Issues.* World Bank Technical Paper 139. Vol. 2. *Sectoral Guidelines.* World Bank Technical Paper 140. Vol. 3. *Guidelines for Environmental Assessment of Energy and Industry Projects.* World Bank Technical Paper 154. Washington, D.C.

_____. 1991b. *The Environmental Challenge.* Selected articles from *Finance and Development.* Washington D.C.

_____. 1991c. *The Forest Sector.* A World Bank Policy Paper. Washington, D.C.

_____. 1991d. *Gender and Poverty in India.* A World Bank Country Study. Washington, D.C.

146

_____. 1991e. *The World Bank and the Environment. A Progress Report, Fiscal 1991*. Washington D.C.

_____. 1992a. *A Strategy for Forest Sector Development in Asia*. World Bank Technical Paper 182. Washington, D.C.

_____. 1992b. *World Development Report 1992. Development and the Environment*. New York: Oxford University Press.

Informal Documents

The following titles, produced by various departments within the World Bank during fiscal 1992, may be obtained by writing directly to the department named.

Ahmed, Sadiq. 1991. "Fiscal Policy for Managing Indonesia's Environment." Policy Research Working Paper 786. World Bank, Asia Regional Office, Country Department V, Washington, D.C.

Altaf, M. A., and J. A. Hughes. 1991. "Willingness to Pay for Improved Sanitation in Ouagadougou, Burkina Faso: A Contingent Valuation Study." World Bank, Infrastructure and Urban Development Department, Washington, D.C.

Altaf, Anjum, Jamal Haroon, and Dale Whittington. 1992. "Households' Willingness to Pay for Water in Rural Areas of the Punjab, Pakistan." Program Report Series. UNDP–World Bank Water and Sanitation Program, Infrastructure and Urban Development Department, Washington, D.C.

American Center for Oriental Research. 1992. "Regional Study on Cultural Heritage in Biologically Diverse Areas: EMENA." World Bank, Environment Department, Assessments and Programs Division, Washington, D.C.

Barnes, Douglas F., and Liu Qian. 1991. "Urban Interfuel Substitution, Energy Use and Equity in Developing Countries: Some Preliminary Results." Prepared for the 1991 International Conference of the International Association for Energy Economics, East-West Center, Honolulu, July 8–10. World Bank, Industry and Energy Department, Washington, D.C.

Bartelmus, Peter, Ernst Lutz, and Stefan Schweinfest. 1992. "Integrated Environmental and Economic Accounting: A Case Study for Papua New Guinea." Environment Working Paper 54. World Bank, Environment Department, Washington, D.C.

Behnke, R. H., and I. Scoones. 1992. "Rethinking Range Ecology: Implications for Rangeland Management in Africa." Environment Working Paper 53. World Bank, Environment Department, Washington, D.C.

Bernstein, Janis D. 1992. "Alternative Approaches to Pollution Control and Waste Management: Regulatory and Economic Instruments." UNDP–World Bank–UNCHS Urban Management Program Discussion Paper 3. World Bank, Infrastructure and Urban Development Department, Washington, D.C.

Bloom, David, David Wheeler, and David Beede. 1991. "Measuring and Explaining Cross-Establishment Variation in the Generation and Management of Industrial Waste." World Bank, Environment Department, Assessments and Programs Division, Washington, D.C.

Bradley, David, Sandy Cairncross, Trudy Harpham, and Carolyn Stephens. 1991. "A Review of Environmental Health Impacts in Developing Country Cities."

UNDP–World Bank–UNCHS Urban Management Program Discussion Paper 6. World Bank, Infrastructure and Urban Development Department, Washington, D.C.

Cleaver, Kevin, and Gotz Schreiber. 1991. "The Population, Environment and Agriculture Nexus in Sub-Saharan Africa." Africa Region Technical Paper. World Bank, Washington, D.C.

Csaki, Csaba. 1992. "Transformation of Agriculture in Central Eastern Europe and the Former USSR: Major Policy Issues and Perspectives." Policy Research Working Paper 888. World Bank, Agriculture and Rural Development Department and Country Economics Department, Washington, D.C.

Dalfeit, A. 1991. "Ecological Constraints to Sustainable Management of the Tropical Moist Forest." Policy and Research Division Working Paper 25. World Bank, Environment Department, Washington, D.C.

Daly, H. 1991. "Ecological Economics and Sustainable Development: From Concept to Policy." Policy and Research Division Working Paper 24. World Bank, Environment Department, Washington, D.C.

Davis, Shelton H. 1991. "Indigenous Views of Land and the Environment." Background paper for *World Development Report 1992*. World Bank, World Development Report office, Washington, D.C.

Ebert, Craig, and Abyd Karmali. 1992. "Uncertainties in Estimating Greenhouse Gas Emissions." Environment Working Paper 52. World Bank, Environment Department, Washington, D.C.

Edwards, Peter. 1992. "Reuse of Human Wastes in Aquaculture." UNDP–World Bank–UNCHS Urban Management Program Discussion Paper 2. World Bank, Infrastructure and Urban Development Department, Washington, D.C.

Eskeland, Gunnar. 1992. "Demand Management in Environmental Protection: Fuel Taxes and Air Pollution in Mexico City." World Bank, Country Economics Department, Washington, D.C.

Faiz, Asif, and José Carbajo. 1991. "Automotive Air Pollution and Control: Strategic Options for Developing Countries." World Bank, Infrastructure and Urban Development Department, Washington, D.C.

Fargeix, André. 1992. "Financing of Pollution Control Programs." World Bank, Europe, Middle East and North Africa Region, Environment Division, Washington, D.C.

Floor, Willem, and Robert van der Plas. 1992. "CO_2 Emissions by the Residential Sector: Environmental Implications of Interfuel Substitution." Energy Series Working Paper 51. World Bank, Industry and Energy Department, Washington, D.C.

Goodland, Robert, Herman Daly, and Salah El Serafy, eds. 1991. "Environmentally Sustainable Economic Development: Building on Brundtland." Environment Working Paper 46. World Bank, Environment Department, Washington, D.C.

Goodland, R., A. Juras, and R. Pachauri. 1991. "Can Hydro-Reservoirs in Tropical Moist Forests Be Made Environmentally Acceptable?" Policy and Research Division Working Paper 23. World Bank, Environment Department, Washington, D.C.

Guggenheim, Scott. 1992. "Common Property and the Rural Poor." World Bank, Environment Department, Assessments and Programs Division, Washington, D.C.

148

Guggenheim, Scott, and Maritta Koch-Weser. 1991. "Participation for Sustainable Development." World Bank, World Development Report office, Washington, D.C.

Hamrin, Robert A. 1991. "The Role of Monitoring and Enforcement in Pollution Control in the U.S." World Bank, Country Economics Department, Washington, D.C.

Harrison, Anne. 1992. "Natural Assets and National Income." Policy and Research Division Working Paper 34. World Bank, Environment Department, Washington, D.C.

Hartwick, J. M., and A. P. Hageman. 1991. "Economic Depreciation of Mineral Stocks and the Contribution of El Serafy." Policy and Research Division Working Paper 27. World Bank, Environment Department, Washington, D.C.

Hazell, Peter. 1991. "Drought, Poverty and the Environment." World Bank, Agricultural Policies Division, Washington, D.C.

Heggie, Ian. 1991. "Improving Management and Charging Policies for Roads: An Agenda for Reform." INU Discussion Paper 92. World Bank, Infrastructure and Urban Development Department, Washington, D.C.

Horton, Mark. 1992. "Cultural Heritage in Biologically Diverse Areas: Sub-Saharan Africa Regional Study." World Bank, Environment Department, Assessments and Programs Division, Washington, D.C.

Huq, Mainul, and David Wheeler. 1992. "Pollution Reduction without Formal Regulation: Evidence from Bangladesh." World Bank, Environment Department, Assessments and Programs Division, Washington, D.C.

Jack, William. 1992. "Power Sharing and Pollution Control: Coordinating Policies Among Levels of Government." Policy Research Working Paper 887. World Bank, Country Economics Department, Washington, D.C.

Joshi, P. K., and N. T. Singh. 1991. "Environment Issues in Relation to Incentive and Resource Allocation in Indian Agriculture." World Bank, Country Economics Department, Trade Policy Division, Washington, D.C., and Central Soil Salinity Research Institute, Karnal (Haryana), India.

Kanbur, Ravi. 1992. "Heterogeneity, Distribution, and Cooperation in Common Property Resource Management." Policy Research Working Paper 844. World Bank, Research Administration Department, Washington, D.C.

Katko, Tapio. 1992. "The Development of Water Supply Associations in Finland and Its Significance for Developing Countries." Water and Sanitation Discussion Paper 8. UNDP–World Bank Water and Sanitation Program, Washington, D.C.

Kaur, Ravinder. 1991. "Women in Forestry in India." Policy Research Working Paper 714. World Bank, Population and Human Resources Department, Women in Development Division, Washington, D.C.

King, Kenneth. 1992. "Financing the Phasing Out of Ozone-Depleting Substances: Issues in the Application of the Incremental Cost Criterion Illustrated by the Case of Egypt." Policy and Research Division Working Paper 32. World Bank, Environment Department, Washington, D.C.

King, Kenneth, and Mohan Munasinghe. 1991. "Incremental Costs of Phasing Out Ozone Depleting Substances." Environment Working Paper 47. World Bank, Environment Department, Washington, D.C.

King, Kenneth, and Mohan Munasinghe. 1992. "Cost-Effective Means to Limit the Emissions of Greenhouse Gases in Developing Countries." Policy and Research Division Working Paper 30. World Bank, Environment Department, Washington, D.C.

Kinnersley, David. 1991. "Privatisation and the Water Environment: A Note on Water Agencies in Britain." Paper presented at the International Workshop on Comprehensive Water Resource Management, June 1991. World Bank, Agriculture and Rural Development Department, Washington, D.C.

Kishor, Nalin M. 1992. "Pesticide Externalities, Comparative Advantage, and Commodity Trade: Cotton in Andhra Pradesh, India." Policy Research Working Paper 928. World Bank, Country Economics Department, Trade Policy Division, Washington, D.C.

Kopp, Raymond J. 1992. "Economic Incentives and Point Source Emissions: Choice of Modeling Platform." Policy Research Working Paper 920. World Bank, Country Economics Department, Public Economics Division, Washington, D.C.

Kreimer, Alcira, and Mohan Munasinghe, eds. 1991. "Managing Natural Disasters and the Environment." Selected Materials from the Colloquium on the Environment and Natural Disaster Management. World Bank, Environment Department, Policy and Research Division, Washington, D.C.

Larsen, Bjorn, and Anwar Shah. 1992a. "Tradeable Carbon Emissions Permits and International Transfers." Presented at the 15th Annual Conference of the International Association of Energy Economics, Tours, France, May 18–20.

_____. 1992b. "World Energy Subsidies and Global Carbon Emissions." World Bank, Country Economics Department, Public Economics Division, Washington, D.C.

Leventhal, Richard M., and Bryan J. Dennis. 1992. "Survey of Biodiversity and Cultural Heritage Sites in Latin America and the Caribbean." World Bank, Environment Department, Assessments and Programs Division, Washington, D.C.

Lopez, Ramon, Ridwan Ali, and Bjorn Larsen. 1991. "How Trade and Economic Policies Affect Agriculture: A Framework for Analysis Applied to Tanzania and Malawi." Policy Research Working Paper 719. World Bank, Southern Africa Department, Washington, D.C.

Lovei, Laszlo, and Dale Whittington. 1991. "Rent Seeking in Water Supply." INU Discussion Paper 85. World Bank, Infrastructure and Urban Development Department, Washington, D.C.

Lusigi, Walter J., and Bengt A. Nekby. 1991. "Dryland Management in Sub-Saharan Africa: The Search for Sustainable Development Options." World Bank, Africa Technical Department, Environment Division, Washington, D.C.

McCarthy, F. Desmond, and Ashok Dhareshwar. 1992. "Economic Shocks and the Global Environment." Policy Research Working Paper 870. World Bank, International Economics Department, Washington, D.C.

Margulis, Sergio. 1992. "Back-of-the-Envelope Estimates of Environmental Damage Costs in Mexico." Policy Research Working Paper 824. World Bank, Latin America and Caribbean Region, Country Department II, Washington, D.C.

Martin, Paul, and others. 1992. "The Industrial Pollution Projection System: Concept, Initial Development and Critical Assessment." World Bank, Environment Department, Assessments and Programs Division, Washington, D.C.

Mathews, Geoffrey. 1992. "Overall Creditworthiness As a Tool for Sustainable Development." Policy and Research Division Working Paper 29. World Bank, Environment Department, Washington, D.C.

Munasinghe, Mohan. 1992. "Environmental Economics and Valuation in Development Decisionmaking." Environment Working Paper 51. World Bank, Environment Department, Washington, D.C.

Munasinghe, Mohan, and Kenneth King. 1991. "Issues and Options in Implementing the Montreal Protocol in Developing Countries." Environment Working Paper 49. World Bank, Environment Department, Washington, D.C.

Norgaard, Richard B. 1992. "Sustainability and the Economics of Assuring Assets for Future Generations." Policy Research Working Paper 832. World Bank, Office of the Regional Vice President, Asia Regional Office, Washington, D.C.

Paul, Samuel. 1991. "The Bank's Work on Institutional Development in Sectors—Emerging Tasks and Challenges." World Bank, Country Economics Department, Public Sector Management and Private Sector Development Division, Washington, D.C.

Peuker, Axel. 1992. "Public Policies and Deforestation: A Case Study of Costa Rica." Regional Studies Program Report 14. World Bank, Latin America and the Caribbean Technical Department, Environment Division, Washington, D.C.

Ravallion, Martin, Guarav Datt, and Shaohua Chen. 1992. "New Estimates of Aggregate Poverty Measures for the Developing World, 1985–89." World Bank, Population and Human Resources Department, Washington, D.C.

Rogers, Peter. 1992. "Comprehensive Water Resources Management: A Concept Paper." Policy Research Working Paper 879. World Bank, Infrastructure and Urban Development Department, Water and Sanitation Division, Washington, D.C.

Shafik, Nemat, and Sushenjit Bandyopadhyay. 1992. "Economic Growth and Environmental Quality: Time-Series and Cross Country Evidence." Policy Research Working Paper 904. World Bank, World Development Report office, Washington, D.C.

Shah, Anwar, and Bjorn Larsen. 1992. "Carbon Taxes, the Greenhouse Effect, and Developing Countries." World Bank, World Development Report office, Washington, D.C.

Smith, Kirk R., Joel N. Swisher, Rebekah Kanter, and Dilip R. Ahuja. 1991. "Indices for a Greenhouse Gas Control Regime That Incorporates Both Efficiency and Equity Goals." Policy and Research Division Working Paper 22. World Bank, Environment Department, Washington, D.C.

Subbarao, Kalanidhi, and Laura Raney. 1992. "Social Gains from Female Education." World Bank, Population and Human Resources Department, Washington, D.C.

Summers, Lawrence H. 1991. "Investing in *All* the People." Paper prepared for the Quad-i-Azam Lecture at the Eighth Annual General Meeting of the Pakistan Society of Development Economists, Islamabad. World Bank, Office of the Vice President, Development Economics, Washington, D.C.

UNDP–World Bank Water and Sanitation Program. 1992a. "Annual Report 1990–91." World Bank, Infrastructure and Urban Development Department, Washington, D.C.

_____. 1991. "Water Supply and Sanitation in Africa: Laying the Foundation for the 1990s." Abidjan Conference Proceedings. 2 vols. World Bank, Infrastructure and Urban Development Department, Washington, D.C.

van der Tak, Herman G. 1991. "Policies and Measures to Implement the Montreal Protocol." Environment Working Paper 48. World Bank, Environment Department, Washington, D.C.

Van Tongeren, Jan, Stefan Schweinfest, Ernst Lutz, Maria Gomez Luna, and Francisco Guillen Martin. 1991. "Integrated Environmental and Economic Accounting—A Case Study for Mexico." Environment Working Paper 50. World Bank, Environment Department, Washington, D.C.

Wachter, Daniel, 1992. "Land Titling for Land Conservation in Developing Countries." Policy and Research Division Working Paper 28. World Bank, Environment Department, Washington, D.C.

Wachter, Daniel, and John English. 1992. "The World Bank's Experience with Rural Land Titling." Policy and Research Division Working Paper 35. World Bank, Environment Department, Washington, D.C.

Wali, Alaka, and Shelton Davis. 1992. "Protecting Amerindian Lands: A Review of World Bank Experience with Indigenous Land Regularization Programs in Lowland South America." Regional Studies Program Report 19. Joint study by World Bank, Environment Department, and Latin America and Caribbean Technical Department, Washington, D.C.

Wells, Michael. 1991 "Trust Funds and Endowments as a Biodiversity Conservation Tool." Policy and Research Division Working Paper 26. World Bank, Environment Department, Washington, D.C.

Wescoat, James L., Jr. 1992. "Integrating Biodiversity Protection and Cultural Heritage Conservation in Asia and the Pacific: A Strategy Document with Case Studies." World Bank, Environment Department, Assessments and Programs Division, Washington, D.C.

Wheeler, David. 1992. "The Economics of Industrial Pollution Control: An International Perspective." Industry Series Paper 55. World Bank, Industry and Energy Department, Washington, D.C.

White, Thomas, and Jon L. Jickling. 1992. "An Economic and Institutional Analysis of Soil and Water Conservation in Haiti." Policy and Research Division Working Paper 33. World Bank, Environment Department, Washington, D.C.

Whittington, Dale, Donald T. Lauria, Albert M. Wright, Kyeongae Choe, Jeffrey A. Hughes, and Venkateswarlu Swarna. 1992. "Household Demand for Improved Sanitation Services: A Case Study of Kumasi, Ghana." Program Report Series. UNDP–World Bank Water and Sanitation Program. World Bank, Infrastructure and Urban Development Department, Washington, D.C.

World Bank. 1991a. "An Evaluation of Improved Biomass Cookstoves Program: Prospects for Success or Failure." Joint ESMAP–UNDP Report. World Bank, Industry and Energy Department, Washington, D.C.

_____.1991b. "Water and Sanitation Sector Review—Issues in Institutional Performance and 1991 Sector Activities, INUWS." World Bank, Infrastructure and Urban Development Department, Washington, D.C.

_____. 1991c. "Water Supply and Sanitation Sector Maintenance: The Costs of Neglect and Options to Improve It." World Bank, Latin America and Caribbean Region Technical Department, Washington, D.C.

_____. 1992a. "Environment and Development in Latin America and the Caribbean: The Role of the World Bank." World Bank, Latin America and Caribbean Region, Washington, D.C.

_____. 1992b. "OED Précis." World Bank, Operations Evaluations Department, Washington, D.C.

_____. 1992c. "Poverty Reduction Handbook." World Bank, Washington, D.C.

_____. 1992d. "The Social Challenge of Biodiversity Conservation Projects." Global Environment Facility office, Washington, D.C.